Teaching Reading and Writing With
Word Walls

by Janiel M. Wagstaff

SCHOLASTIC
PROFESSIONAL BOOKS

New York • Toronto • London • Auckland • Sydney
Mexico City • New Delhi • Hong Kong

Dedication

To my colleagues who, like me, "find it hard to be satisfied with Things As They Are!"
(from *The Most Wonderful Doll in the World,* Phyllis McGinley, 1950)

. . . .

Acknowledgments

Thanks to Wendy Murray and Terry Cooper of Scholastic Professional Books for their belief in my ideas and their ongoing encouragement.

Thanks to my students—each and every one!

Thanks to my fellow teachers, researchers, and writers for their inspirational voices.

Thanks to my family and friends—especially Mom—"Patience and courage!"

Thanks to those who waited!

Cover design by Kathy Massaro
Cover photograph by Ellen Senisi
Interior design by Grafica Inc.
Photographs on pages 1,12,14,26,107 by Ellen Senisi; all others courtesy of the author.

ISBN 0–590–10390–3

Contents

Dear Colleague,

During the final stretches of completing this book, I occasionally connected to America Online as a diversion to the sometimes difficult task of writing. To my surprise, there were a number of messages in various educational sites that referred to Word Walls. They are mentioned on bulletin boards on balanced literacy, spelling, phonics, and whole language. Apparently, many teachers are becoming aware of these valuable tools and are recommending them to others. While no one method works for everything, Word Walls have been used to bolster reading/language arts programs in the areas of phonics, spelling, and language conventions.

If you teach primary grade students, remedial students, or second-language learners, you will appreciate the practical, literature-based suggestions I provide in the book for teaching skills and strategies. The ideas come from my classroom practice with young learners and have been informed by extensive research into reading and writing processes. I know Word Walls will support your students in becoming better readers and writers and you'll want to continue incorporating them in your classroom practice for years to come!

Janiel Wagstaff

Janiel Wagstaff

Introduction

How do you answer the "back to basics" cry in education? In my classroom, it is easy to find evidence that I value and teach the basics such as phonics, spelling, and language conventions—it's all over the walls.

I am not referring to commercially-prepared charts, bulletin boards, or teaching aides; rather, my students and I collaboratively build Word Walls as we learn and practice phonics, spelling, and language conventions in the context of authentic reading and writing activities. The Walls support ongoing literacy development and are used as helpful references during daily reading and writing.

This Word Wall shows how a literature-rich classroom values phonics and spelling.

My first teaching experiences helped me form core beliefs about the nature of language learning and teaching. My students had trouble transferring learning from contrived, paper-and-pencil tasks to authentic reading and writing tasks. Like others who began this way, I made changes. I started teaching *through language*, realizing that what I needed to teach was right there in the context of what we read and wrote every day in my classroom.

Why Word Walls?

Word Walls serve as permanent records of students' language learning.

With so much research supporting explicit, systematic teaching of phonics (Adams, 1990), educators must be accountable for what takes place

> *"The problem for teachers and those who design instructional materials is how to provide for skill instruction and skill reinforcement within meaning-making activities."*
>
> —Squire, 1994, p. 285

during context-driven lessons. Building and using Word Walls is a logical method to track and extend skill and strategy learning from reading/writing contexts. It is easy to see where a class has been—and determine where they are going—based on the words already on the Wall. For example:

- The number of letters and letter-sound correspondences explicitly covered and practiced with a class is documented by the growth of the ABC Wall.

- The "chunks," or spelling patterns, supporting decoding and spelling are contained on the Chunking Wall.

- High-frequency words are collected on the Words-We-Know Wall.

- Keys to help students remember and use language conventions are documented on the Help Wall.

Anyone entering a classroom with growing Word Walls such as these will feel confident that skills and strategies are being taught regularly in a purposeful fashion.

Word Walls provide ongoing support for varied language learners.

Students progress at different rates and need varied amounts of support as they learn skills and strategies. Learning the letter *S* during "S week" in kindergarten, remembering a spelling pattern beyond the Monday–Friday spelling routine in first grade, or mastering contractions during one second grade unit is not enough for many learners. Rather, students need ongoing support and multiple demonstrations before they incorporate skills and strategies into their reading and writing repertoires.

Word Walls help children develop critical reading and writing skills and strategies and provide ongoing support. Students who are struggling may refer to the Walls for immediate help. It's not unlike the way I set up children for success in guided reading. After the book is introduced and the group is ready to read independently, I say, "Now go ahead and read at your own pace. If you need help, I'll be here to help you." I lean in and listen as children read, cueing and prompting when appropriate. Word Walls are another way of saying: ***Help is right here for you, this is a safe place to learn***.

Any of the Walls can be made more interactive if library pockets are affixed under word categories where they may be reached by students. On the Chunking Wall, for example, a library pocket under the "a" chunks may contain word cards with the "a" chunks from the wall. Students can take specific cards right to their desks to aid spelling or decoding while the Wall stays intact for everyone to use. When finished, the card is replaced in the pocket.

Word Walls enhance learning through practical use.

Many teachers have Word Walls of one kind or another but don't use them to their full advantage. It is important to distinguish between *having* a Word Wall and really *using* a Word Wall. The "just stick it on a wall" approach doesn't work. Actively involving students with the contents of Word Walls does.

There are two primary ways to use Word Walls. First, wordplay activities related to the Walls promote automaticity with letter–sound correspondences, spelling patterns or chunks, high-frequency words, and language conventions. Second, ongoing demonstrations of how to use the Walls promote application of skills and strategies in real reading and writing situations. Daily demonstrations help children learn *how*, *when*, and *why* to apply the skills and strategies they are learning. Providing multiple demonstrations and opportunities to use and practice skills and strategies are two conditions identified as critical to literacy learning (Cambourne, 1988; 1995).

Using references is a real world strategy.

We all use references in our daily lives. We call upon dictionaries and spell-checkers to confirm spelling, thesauruses to aid word choices. Using Word Walls acts as a reference that enables students to more readily solve reading/writing problems independently. Successful independent problem solving diminishes reliance on the teacher and increases a student's self-confidence.

Building and using Word Walls is easily integrated into daily literacy activities.

Word Walls are not created in isolation of other reading and writing activities; rather, they are references for some of what is learned and practiced during these activities. The Word Walls described in this book are created to support the learning of phonics, spelling, and language conventions. (Please note that I do not mean to imply that they are references for *all* that is learned or taught during reading and writing activities.)

The impetus for building the Walls is shared reading and writing. Skills and strategies are supported by use of the Walls during modeled, guided, and independent reading and writing activities. These elements are already part of the balanced literacy programs teachers put into place daily. Thus, Word Walls are not add-ons. They also should not take an inordinate amount of time to build or use. Short, focused wordplay sessions and quick demonstrations are best.

How Are Word Walls Built?

Word Walls are not just decor for the classroom, something to put up and take down with the seasons. They are works in progress. Word Walls are built over time as words are harvested, or taken, from meaningful contexts. These contexts may include shared reading materials such as Big Books, poems, rhymes, or chants. Another context may be oral language experiences such as learning and dramatizing nursery rhymes. Daily news, stories created by the class during interactive writing sessions, and morning messages written by the teacher (Routman, 1991) also provide rich sources for word selection.

The Word Wall building process is very different from putting up an alphabet frieze before the school year begins. I begin the year *anticipating* which Walls may be needed. Walls are readied to be filled with references that I add with students based on common-language experiences. In September, the Walls have few words. Week by week, more words and references are added. By year's end, we have Walls with multiple, meaningful references.

My students and I *collaboratively* select words for the Wall. At first, I assume most of the responsibility for choosing appropriate words, while students come to know how the Walls are constructed and what purposes they serve. Then, students gradually take ownership in selecting Word Wall content.

Children have natural tendencies to search for things that have personal meaning (Routman, 1991). Harvesting words from shared language experiences and maintaining dual ownership of word selection with students make Word Wall words more meaningful.

How Many Words Are Needed?

The number of words chosen at one time to place on the Wall depends on students' comfort levels. In kindergarten, my students and I choose two or three words to add to our ABC Wall each week. In second grade, we choose five words each week to add to our Chunking Wall. Generally, words are chosen on Monday, practiced and reviewed throughout the week, and added to the Walls on Friday. No matter what the time frame, words should be familiar before they are added to the Walls.

Only key words are added to the Walls. Key words are the words harvested, or taken, from the material children read. When building a Chunking Wall, for example, all words generated for the *-an* chunk are not listed on the Wall. Such an approach would result in a cluttered Wall, making it hard for students to reference. Instead, only the *-an* word taken from the poem, rhyme, or chant used to harvest it

> **"What seems to be needed is greater awareness of teacher strategies that can provide instruction or guidance with individual words or word parts within a total context."**
>
> —Squire, 1994, p. 285

should be affixed to the Wall. The effect will be an organized Wall, which reinforces students' strategic use of key words.

Word Walls Within the Balanced Literacy Program

Word Wall activities are generally embedded in daily reading and writing experiences. Shared oral language and reading and writing activities form the context from which Word Wall words are harvested. Wordplay occurs once words are chosen as a means of developing familiarity. Further shared, guided, and independent reading and writing provide children opportunities to apply their developing skills and strategies. The following instructional sequence is typical:

1. First, a shared language context is established through repeated shared readings of a poem, rhyme, or chant, or through shared writing.

2. The Word Wall word(s) is chosen and then taken out of context for explicit examination and wordplay. For example, we may search classroom books for words with a specific letter pattern or build words with the pattern using letter cards.

3. The word(s) is then put back into context, demonstrating how the part fits into the whole. Finishing with another shared reading of the poem, rhyme, or chant focuses attention back on meaning-making. This *whole, part, whole* process keeps learning contextualized. (See Figure 1.)

Children gain critical understandings of the functionality of reading and writing while they learn about the form of language. These understandings are then applied and practiced through continued reading and writing in the content areas during the day.

Naturally, ongoing assessment plays an important role in this process. Ongoing observation and diagnosis shape our literacy lessons. Thus, the literacy context to establish, the number of words to use, the amount of wordplay, and when to add words to a Wall, depend on how students are performing.

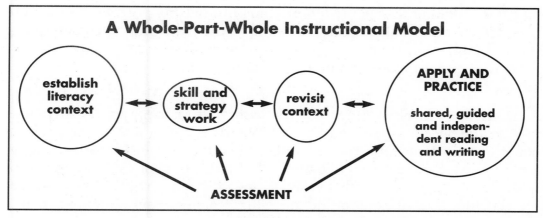

figure 1

The Chicken Before the Egg?

Teachers often ask how children can be expected to read and write before many skills have been learned. "How can they read or write if they don't know their letters? Don't these Walls need to be built first to give children the skills they need to get started?" In fact, basic skills and strategies are best learned while children at emergent levels are engaged in writing and reading using developmentally appropriate materials and activities.

In kindergarten, I want my students to learn letter names, letter forms, and letter-sound correspondences. Toward that end, we work together to build an ABC Wall based on our shared literacy experiences. However, this is not the only goal I have for my students. They need to develop understandings of why we read and write and the joys of these processes. They need to be exposed to multiple reading and writing genres and become motivated as literacy users (Guthrie & Wigfield, 1997; Gambrell, 1996). These goals are attained when purposeful, functional approaches are taken to reading and writing. Programs that focus solely on building requisite skills may leave learners without the understanding of how to apply their learning.

> *"The process of reading cannot be divided into key and support activities. All of its component knowledge and skills must work together within a single integrated and interdependent system. And it is in that way that they must be acquired as well."*
>
> —Adams, 1990, p. 423

For a person learning to play baseball, batting practice is an important part of learning how to play the game. However, imagine a person who has never seen a baseball game. Making that person do nothing but batting practice may lead to the misconception that baseball is about standing at the plate and repeatedly swinging at the ball. That person would miss the purpose of baseball and would think it a boring way to spend an afternoon (Stahl, 1992 p. 620).

If students are to be involved in reading and writing from the start, teachers need to acknowledge and accept approximations (Cambourne, 1988; 1995). They need to understand the developmental characteristics of young literacy learners. And, yes, they need to provide a great deal of support. In early childhood classrooms, especially at the beginning of the school year, we spend the majority of time in shared language activities so that appropriate modeling, teaching, and scaffolding can occur. Still, students have independent time to capitalize on choice and practice.

Over time, as students' knowledge grows, the amount of support and time spent in shared activities shifts toward independent reading and writing modes (Fountas and Pinnell, 1996). This is where teaching becomes an art. Decisions about how much time to spend in shared and guided activities; how much modeling, teaching, and scaffolding to provide; and which materials will furnish the right amount of support and challenge are not clear cut. Often, decisions must be adjusted based on how children respond to instruction. Yet we persist in providing the right type of real reading and writing experiences because we know, no matter how cliché, children learn to read and write by reading and writing. We must simply and expertly provide key help along the way. Creating and using Word Walls is one method for providing that help.

What Makes Word Walls Work?

Although there is no one right way, I've found the following principles important to building and using Word Walls successfully.

"Phonological awareness, letter recognition facility, familiarity with spelling patterns, spelling-sound relations, and individual words must be developed in concert with real reading and real writing with deliberate reflection on the forms, functions, and meanings of texts."

—Adams, 1990, p. 422

- *Word Walls should be built over time with shared ownership between teacher and students.*

The more involved students are, the more likely they are to use the Walls purposefully.

- *Words are harvested from rich language contexts.*

Don't just slap up a list of words. Know your purpose for each Wall and look for words in real literacy contexts that will serve that purpose.

- *Word Walls should be kept as simple and uncluttered as possible.*

Be choosy about what goes on your Walls. Use key words. One word, not a whole list, should represent a sound or spelling pattern (chunk).

- *Words on the Walls should be visible to everyone.*

As references, the words on the Walls must be clearly visible, even from the back of the room. I write the words on different colored cards in large letters with bold black marker. Cutting around the configuration of each word makes them more distinguishable (Cunningham, 1995).

A first grader brainstorms words that contain the est chunk.

• *What to build and when to add is based on student needs. Walls must be kept developmentally appropriate.*

The grade level suggestions made in the following chapters are based on generalizations of what kids know, what they need, and when they need it. You will know best the type of Word Walls that are appropriate for your class.

• *Use of Walls as helpful references must be modeled.*

Don't just use Word Walls for wordplay aimed at having students learn certain letters or words. Aim for practical use of the Walls in real literacy situations. Achieve this by modeling, modeling, and more modeling. You can't model enough! Show your students how to use the references on the Wall during shared and guided reading and writing. Think aloud about your use of the Walls, and allow students to share their experiences using the Walls.

• *The goal of creating and using Word Walls is ultimately automaticity of basic processes.*

Use of the Walls in multiple contexts combined with a daily regimen of reading and writing will assist in the development of students' automaticity with skills covered on the Walls. Since automaticity of basic skills and processes is critical to fluent reading and writing, time is appropriately spent on its development.

Finally, as you read this book keep in mind that the grade levels and time frames associated with particular Word Walls are only suggestions. As educators, our greatest source of information for making developmentally appropriate instructional decisions comes from our observations of students at work. I hope you will freely adapt these techniques to provide the kind of support your students need.

> **"While the message in the text is always the goal, attending to parts of the text is acceptable, temporarily, in service of that goal."**
>
> —Clay, 1991, p. 143

CHAPTER ONE

The ABC Wall

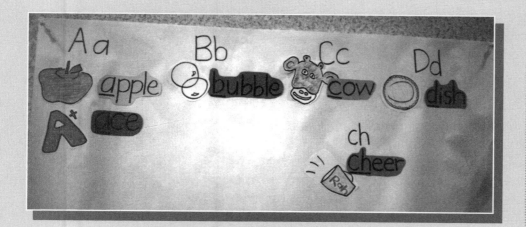

> " Letter of the week or no letter of the week, that is the question. "

The ABC Wall is a tool for learning the alphabet. It consists of one key word for each consonant. For example, the word *feet* may represent the letter *f* and two key words representing the long and short sounds of each vowel (i.e., *apron* for long *a* and *apple* for short *a*). Words representing the hard and soft sounds of consonants such as *c* and *g* and common digraphs such as *sh, ch, wh,* and *th* can also be added.

The ABC Wall is built with beginning readers and writers to learn letter forms, letter names, and basic letter-sound correspondences. This knowledge is used and expanded throughout the day during reading and writing activities. For example, students are encouraged to use key words on the ABC Wall to make connections to new words when reading emergent reading materials or when spelling words while writing stories. This strategy capitalizes on moving from the known to the new.

I developed the idea for the ABC Wall as an alternative to the typical letter-of-the-week format used in many kindergarten classrooms (Wagstaff, 1997). I was troubled by the slow pace of letter-of-the-week instruction and the isolated manner in which letters were taught. I wanted a practical way to introduce letters and sounds at a faster pace, grounded in real literacy activities. I also wanted students to see the learning of letters as keys to reading and writing.

A first grader writes a story.

Choosing just two key words a week from an enjoyable shared reading experience doubles the pace of letter-of-the-week instruction. Students are capable of learning at this pace, and even faster, as long as appropriate support is provided through wordplay and continual use of the ABC Wall. Working from a shared reading context keeps the learning of letters and their corresponding sounds grounded in reading—the context in which this learning will be used. Therefore, building and using an ABC Wall allows classroom activities to revolve around reading and writing, not around learning letters.

GETTING STARTED

Purposes of the ABC Wall

I've used the ABC Wall in kindergarten and first grade classrooms to:

- introduce students to the alphabet
- increase students' phonemic awareness
- help students recognize and write letter forms
- build students' automatic recognition of letters and sounds
- build students' knowledge of letter–sound correspondences
- promote students' use of initial and final letter cues in reading and spelling

The two primary goals of the ABC Wall are to develop students' phonemic awareness and automaticity with basic letter-sound correspondences. Phonemic awareness, or the awareness that words are composed of sounds, involves the ability to perceive and manipulate sounds in spoken words. It is important because, if children have difficulty hearing, producing, and manipulating sounds in words, they will have difficulty reading and writing words and letters associated with those sounds. Imagine how hard it would be to represent music with notes if you had trouble hearing the pitch and length of sounds in a musical piece. Likewise, students who cannot perceive or segment sounds in spoken words, such as the /k/ sound in *cat*, experience difficulty representing sounds with letters. In *Beginning to Read: Thinking and Learning About Print*, Marilyn Jager Adams concludes that phonemic awareness is "the single most powerful determinant" of successful reading and writing development. Blending sounds to form words and segmenting sounds to write words, as well as other oral language activities associated with the ABC Wall, increase students' phonemic awareness.

By first grade, students should also be able to quickly and effortlessly recognize and name the letters of the alphabet in random order and have a working knowledge of basic letter–sound correspondences. Automaticity is critical. These abilities enable children to move successfully through the developmental stages of reading and writing toward fluency.

Building the ABC Wall

I begin each week with a literacy activity, such as reading aloud a favorite nursery rhyme. This rhyme serves as the source of words for the ABC Wall. Key words for the ABC Wall are chosen on the strength of their beginning sounds, since children will use these cues to make connections to new words. Words beginning with single consonants are added to the ABC Wall first; later, we add words beginning with consonant digraphs. Picture cues may accompany ABC Wall words to lend secondary support to beginners. Words are chosen on Monday, their beginning sounds practiced and reviewed through-out the week. Word cards containing the words are added to the Wall on Friday. Words are put on the Wall in alphabetical order.

Let's look at a typical lesson for building the ABC Wall. In your own classroom, of course, you will want to tailor this to the needs and abilities of your students.

BEGINNING OF WEEK

SAMPLE LESSON

Adding to the ABC Wall (Lesson Routine)

A. Read aloud a rhyme, poem, chant, or song.

B. Choose key words.

C. Develop phonemic awareness.

D. Associate sounds with letters (phonics).

E. Practice letter formation.

F. Revisit the rhyme throughout the week.

A. *Read aloud a rhyme, poem, chant or song.*

I begin by writing the chant "Let's Get the Rhythm" in large print on poster paper. When preparing a chart for emergent readers, I often include picture cues. On this poster, pictures can be added for the body parts.

I have several reasons for opening with "Let's Get the Rhythm." First, I want to focus on the letters *f, g,* and *h.* This chant contains strong model words beginning with each of these letters. Second, despite the length, the rhythm and repetition make the chant easy to learn. Certainly, shorter chants and rhymes are more appropriate at the beginning of the year with emergent readers. Third, the move-ment involved in the chant encourages children to be active learners and makes the experience game-like. Additionally, the chant's content relates to the science cur-riculum (body parts).

Let's Get the Rhythm
A chant adapted by Anne Miranda (Scholastic, 1994)

Let's get the rhythm of the game. Snap, snap.

Now you've got the rhythm of the game. Snap, snap.

Let's get the rhythm of the hands. Clap, clap.

Now you've got the rhythm of the hands. Clap, clap.

Let's get the rhythm of the feet. Stamp, stamp.

Now you've got the rhythm of the feet. Stamp, stamp.

Let's get the rhythm of the hips. Swing, swing.

Now you've got the rhythm of the hips. Swing, swing.

Let's get the rhythm of the knees. Slap, slap.

Now you've got the rhythm of the knees. Slap, slap.

Let's get the rhythm of the head. Shake, shake.

Now you've got the rhythm of the head. Shake, shake.

Now you've got the rhythm of the game!

I recite the chant to my class. The children catch on, learning it orally. As we sing the chant again, we add movements. Then I call students' attention to the print. We focus on the one-to-one correspondence of words and sentences. Volunteers point to lines as we read. Students become more adept with one-to-one matching and other concepts of print as they acquire more and more experience.

I then call attention to other aspects of print by using word frames, highlighters, Wikki Stix®, or Post-it® tape. For example, I may frame the word *the* because it is a word already posted on our Words-We-Know Wall (Chapter 3). I may use a pointer to note the word-space-word-space pattern of the print (reinforcing the concept of word) and to count letters in a few words (reinforcing the concept of letter). These introductory or review teaching points should occur frequently and remain brief. Be careful not to cover too many points. Keep in mind there are many opportunities to highlight print features throughout the day.

B. *Choose key words.*

After playing with the print a bit, my students and I look for appropriate ABC Wall words. I refer to this as "harvesting" key words. When this process begins, I take most of the responsibility for choosing words, then gradually involve the students more and more as they understand the purpose of the ABC Wall. The following dialogue illustrates how we choose words for the Wall.

Teacher: Now that we know "Let's Get the Rhythm" pretty well, let's look closely at some of the words so we can add them to our ABC Wall. I heard a word that begins like *food, fudge,* and *favorite.* We need a word for the /f/ sound on our ABC Wall to help us read and write other words with /f/. Did you hear a word that begins with /f/?

Students: Feet!

(If they have trouble identifying the word, help the children orally segment the /f/ sound in *food, fudge,* and *favorite.* Then reread the chant, asking children to listen for words that begin with that sound.)

Teacher: Yes, the word *feet* (framing the word on the reading poster) starts with /f/, the first sound in *food, fudge,* and *favorite.* Watch as I write *feet* on a card. (See Figure 2.) It begins with the letter *f.* We will work on learning the letter *f* and its sound, /f/. Who would like to draw a picture of feet to put on the ABC Wall along with our word card?

figure 2

Using the same procedure, students identify other key words by listening for particular beginning sounds (in this case /g/ and /h/). Since this chant contains several words beginning with /h/, student ownership is increased by allowing them to select which /h/ word they would like to add to the Wall. The key words for /g/ and /h/ are written on colorful cards which will be affixed to the ABC Wall after practice throughout the week with these sounds and their corresponding letters. A student-generated picture cue may accompany each word card.

C. Develop phonemic awareness.

Once the key words (*game, hands,* and *feet*) are chosen, I continue to build phonemic awareness by focusing on their beginning sounds. For example, I may read aloud a list of words and ask students to identify which have the same beginning sound as one of the key words. Connections are then made to each sound's corresponding letter.

D. Associate sounds with letters (phonics).

Teacher: The words *game, hands,* and *feet* will make great additions to our ABC Wall because they will remind us of letters and sounds in words we read and write. Read each word with me.

(The students and I read each word as I hold up the word card. If students have trouble, return to another shared reading of the chant. Have students match each card to its corresponding word in the chant.)

Teacher: Listen carefully to the sound this word begins with: *game, g-g-g-g-game.* The sound is /g/.

(NOTE: The word *game* will represent the hard sound of *g.* A word representing the soft sound of *g* (/j/ as in *giant*) may be added at another time based on a different reading experience.)

Teacher: The letter *g* often stands for the sound we hear at the beginning of the word *game.* Listen to other words that start with /g/: *gate, ghost, gas, garage.* What is the sound?

Teacher & Students: /g/

Teacher: Give a thumbs up or thumbs down sign for each word I say. Does it start with /g/ like *game?* Does it begin with the letter *g?*

(I say several words, one at a time. Some begin with /g/; others do not. Students give a response signal after each word, and we discuss the responses.)

Teacher: Can you think of other words that begin with /g/ like the word *game?*

Teacher & Students: Get, gotcha', goof . . .

(If a word is volunteered that does not begin with /g/, ask students to repeat the word slowly, listening for the beginning sound. This can be modeled for additional help. For example, reiterate or stretch the initial sound in the word. Together, identify the beginning sound. If a word is volunteered that is spelled with *g* but stands for the /j/ sound, such as *gym*, have students note the difference in the beginning sound but state that the word is spelled with the letter *g*. Let them know that words with both *g* sounds will be represented on your Wall.)

E. *Practice letter formation.*

After the phonemic awareness and phonics activities, I have my students practice letter formation.

Teacher: Let's work on *writing* the letter *g*. See how it looks at the beginning of the word *game?* Let's make a *g* in the air.

(The students and I make the letter *g* in the air with our fingers. I may point out the parts of the letter and how these relate to other known letters. For example, "Circle around like an *o,* then draw a line down and curve around like a *j."*

Talk continues as letter formation is modeled on an overhead projector or chalkboard.)

Teacher: Now let's try it again. Write the letter *g*. It is important to know how to write the letter *g* so that when you hear words with /g/ and see words with *g*, you will know how to write and read them.

Students then write the letter *g* on individual chalkboards or scratch paper. I monitor and provide assistance as needed. Capital letter formation may also be introduced and practiced. While students are practicing letter formation, I ask them to volunteer words that begin with the /g/ sound. This keeps everyone engaged.

Meeting Individual Needs

To meet individual needs, I encourage students who are ready to write word parts or whole words instead of individual letters.

Following a few minutes of practice, I continue with the other letters. I ask students to listen for the beginning sound in the word *hands* and then *feet*. Words with like beginning sounds are volunteered and letter formation is practiced.

F. Revisit the rhyme throughout the week.

We follow these activities with one last choral reading of "Let's Get the Rhythm" and proceed to reading workshop.

What Is Reading Workshop?

During reading workshop, students have many reading options. They can read and explore books of different genres and on a variety of topics. They can also read books (in their book boxes) and respond to them in their journals. In addition, they can visit literacy centers. While students are engaged in these activities, I meet with a homogeneous reading group for a guided reading session.

Things to Remember

- Lessons for creating Word Walls are fast-paced, reserving significant classroom time for extended reading and writing. Harvesting words at the beginning of the week takes more time than review activities do throughout the week. Investing this initial time pays off. Once the letters and sounds are introduced, more practice and review is possible through multiple contexts.

- As mentioned, I tend to organize instruction around one-week time frames. *Monday:* Harvest key words from the rhyme, poem, chant, or song. *Tuesday through Thursday:* Review and practice the sound-letter correspondences. *Friday:* Place word cards containing each key word on the ABC Wall.

- Before words are added to the ABC Wall on Friday, they should be very familiar to students. If students are still struggling, devote more time to review and practice or, in the future, harvest fewer key words each week. Likewise, if the pace seems too slow, begin the week by choosing more key words.

- As the week's activities unfold, many words with the target beginning sounds will be generated. Remember to add only the key words to the ABC Wall. This will aid students' memory, encourage strategy use, and prevent the ABC Wall from becoming a cluttered, hard-to-use mess!

MID-WEEK PRACTICE ACTIVITIES

Throughout the week, we revisit "Let's Get the Rhythm" and our ABC Wall words—*game, hands,* and *feet.* Here are some ways students work with these words and their corresponding beginning sounds and letters. The practice activities are easily adaptable to any target letters. Extensive amounts of time need not be spent on these activities. Students will continue to develop automaticity with letters and sounds over time through continuous use of the ABC Wall during reading and writing.

- **Picture Hunt:** Students hunt for objects or pictures of objects whose names begin with /g/, /h/, and /f/. These objects and pictures are placed in a learning center where students will sort them into /g/, /h/, and /f/ groups according to beginning sounds.

- **Sound Books:** Students make individual sound books, sorting prepared picture cards into /g/, /h/, and /f/ piles, then stapling each pile into a separate book.

- **Letter Formation:** Students practice letter formation on chalkboards, scratch paper, and in learning centers filled with sandboxes, shaving cream, and other kinesthetic writing materials.

- **Letter Sort:** Students sort upper- and lowercase letter cards written in different fonts or print styles.

- **Magnetic Words:** Students make key words with magnetic letters or letter cards, mix the letters, and then reform the words.

- **Word Hunt:** Students hunt for *g, h,* and *f* words in classroom books and in their writing. They add the words to class posters. (See Figure 3.) Later, posters can be bound into a big ABC book.

- **Morning Message:** Students circle words that begin with target letters in the Morning Message.

- **Frame Words:** Students frame words beginning with target letters during shared reading.

figure 3

- **Mask It:** Students predict /g/, /h/, and /f/ words that I mask while reading Big Books, chants, rhymes, and so forth.

- **Word Sort:** Students sort collected *g*, *h*, and *f* words (written on index cards) in a sorting center.

- **Letter Books:** Students make individual-letter books by sorting prepared word cards into *g*, *h*, and *f* piles and then stapling each pile into a separate book.

- **Label It:** Students label classroom items whose names begin with *g*, *h*, and *f*.

- **Word Match:** Students match the key word cards to the reading poster during reading workshop.

- **Writing Workshop:** Students orally segment words and record letters as they write during shared, interactive, or independent writing.

- **Sentence Strips:** Students reread the chant from sentence strips and/or word cards in a pocket chart. They take the words or sentences, mix them up, and reorder them.

- **Reread New Favorites:** We call the rhyme of the week our *New Favorite*. Students receive a copy to keep in their *favorites folder* for rereading. Students reread their personal copies of the chant individually, in small groups, and at home. Rereading is an important part of a balanced literacy program for emerging and developing readers. It builds fluency, confidence, and sight–word recognition. If the New Favorite is too long for successful independent rereading, students are given a shorter, modified version. (See Figure 4.) Students enjoy taking their favorites folders home each week to show off their growing reading skills!

Let's get the rhythm of the game!

Let's get the rhythm of the game.
Snap, snap.
Now you've got the rhythm
of the game. Snap, snap.

Let's get the rhythm of the hands.
Clap, clap.
Now you've got the rhythm of the
hands. Clap, clap.

Let's get the rhythm of the feet.
Stamp, stamp.
Now you've got the rhythm of the
feet. Stamp, stamp.

figure 4

● **Practice Pages:** Our *g, h,* and *f* ABC Wall words and their beginning letter–sound correspondences are also reviewed on *practice pages.* (See Figure 5.) Students fold the page on the dotted line to hide the picture clues. They read these pages individually or with partners, saying the letter name and reading each key word. If help is needed, students can peek at the picture clues. This short review activity is aimed at building automaticity with letter–sound correspondences and reinforcing memory of key words. Practice pages may be sent home for review and then returned to school. They can be stored in a *practice folder* and reviewed as new pages are added.

"**We look at it to spell things.**"

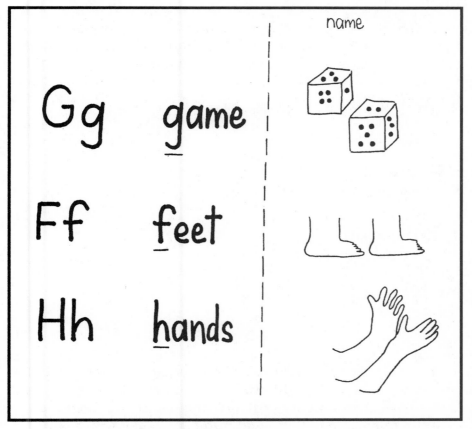

figure 5

END OF WEEK

Once I am confident my students are sufficiently familiar with the key words and their beginning letter-sounds, we add the cards to the ABC Wall. This usually occurs on Friday. Students point out where the cards go on the Wall (alphabetical order) and the picture cue is added.

Tips on Choosing the Best Rhymes

- On the first day of school—even in kindergarten—I want my students to see themselves as readers and writers. I choose poems that are familiar or particularly short in length to begin building both literacy concepts and our ABC Wall. For example, I recently began the kindergarten year with the familiar nursery rhyme "Jack and Jill." We recited the rhyme, dramatized it, and read it in Big Book form and on a shared reading poster. Students made their own copies to read and reread. These copies were sent home at the end of the week. Additional copies were added to their book boxes for rereading. We used the context of "Jack and Jill" to add the letters *j* (for Jack), *p* (for pail), and *w* (for water) to our ABC Wall.

- Consider the potential of even very short chants or jump rope rhymes. They enable beginners to feel great success while boosting phonemic awareness and building the same literacy concepts (like one-to-one matching and directionality) that may be covered with longer material. One of my kindergartners' favorites was "The Bubble Gum Game."

The Bubble Gum Game

Bubble gum, bubble gum,
in a dish.
How many pieces
do you wish?

Reciting this rhyme became a favorite transition and gym time game. After chanting in a circle, students threw a soft ball back and forth, counting catches until the ball was dropped. In class, we tallied the number of catches on a chart. We used the chart to review the purpose of tallying, counting, and numbers, along with math

Kindergarten and first graders love to read and reread shared reading charts of favorite poems, rhymes and chants.

concepts such as predicting (based on our previous records) and greater than and less than. With a little creative thinking, even the shortest chant may lend itself to important cross-curricular connections!

The bubble gum chant, short as it was, enabled us to add *bubble* as our key *b* word and *gum* as our key *g* word to the ABC Wall. As with other poems, rhymes, and chants, we spent a week rereading and revisiting the chant on a shared reading poster, and practiced the key words and letters during wordplay before adding them to our ABC Wall. The fun of "The Bubble Gum Game" was long lasting, providing many opportunities for rereading and reviewing key sounds, words, and letters. My students sure knew *b* and *g* in a hurry! I learned to notice any chant, rhyme, song, or rhythm they used during free time or on the playground, thus capitalizing on their natural language and interests. Tunes from commercials that became "stuck in our heads" were also rich sources for favorites. Along the way, my kindergartners have taught me a few new rhymes and rhythms!

● There are many terrific sources of interactive rhymes. Following are some books that I recommend.

Brown, M. (1985). *Hand Rhymes.* New York: Penguin.

—. (1987). *Play Rhymes.* New York: Penguin.

Cole, J. (1989). *Anna Banana: 101 Jump-Rope Rhymes.* New York: Scholastic.

Cole, J. & Calmenson, S. (1990). *Miss Mary Mack and Other Children's Street Rhymes.* New York: Scholastic.

—. (1991). *The Eentsy, Weentsy Spider: Fingerplays and Action Rhymes.* New York: Scholastic.

Moore, H. (1997). *A Poem a Day: 180 Thematic Poems and Activities That Teach and Delight All Year Long.* New York: Scholastic.

Poetry Place Anthology. (1983). New York: Scholastic.

Two students read aloud "Bubble Gum, Bubble Gum."

Connecting the ABC Wall to Reading and Writing

Once we have started the ABC Wall, I begin showing my students how to use the words when reading and writing. The following are two lessons that demonstrate how I connect the ABC Wall to authentic reading and writing experiences.

SAMPLE LESSON

Using the ABC Wall During Writing

I frequently demonstrate how the beginning sounds in key words on the ABC Wall are helpful in spelling other meaningful words. These demonstrations are brief. Their power is in their frequency. If student attention is waning, or time for the lesson is running short, I simply model aloud rather than engaging students in a teacher-student response dialogue. The process of orally segmenting words and referring to the ABC Wall for help in recording the letters in the words should take place with only a few words, so it is not exhausting and attention can be given to other matters of composing text. A short amount of time can be spent on modeling every day until a piece is completed. I publish many of my stories, thereby modeling the whole writing process. These stories often become class favorites, frequently checked out for independent reading and home sharing.

Using the ABC Wall During Writing (Lesson Routine)

A. Think aloud about a topic for writing.

B. Focus on an important word related to the topic.

C. Associate the word's beginning sound with its corresponding letter, and refer to the ABC Wall.

D. Write the letter. (If appropriate, continue to orally segment the word, relating sounds to letters and referring to the ABC Wall for help in recording letters.)

E. Evaluate the spelling attempt.

F. Continue thinking aloud and adding to the piece.

A. Think aloud about a topic for writing.

Teacher: My husband, John, and I were lucky when we moved to Maryland because we found a little house so quickly. We were worried that it would be hard to find a place to live, and we would be stuck with a big moving truck full of furniture. The little house we found is white with green awnings and has a grassy yard with big shade trees in back. My cats love to run around the yard, and Snydley even climbs the trees.

B. Focus on an important word related to the topic.

Teacher: I think finding our house would make a good story idea. I know a lot about it, since it is something that happened to me. If I choose to write a story about our new little house, how might I begin to write the word *house?* Let's say *house* slowly together. What sound do you hear at the beginning of the word?

Students: /h/

C. Associate the word's beginning sound with its corresponding letter, and refer to the ABC Wall.

Teacher: Right! The word *house* begins like our new ABC Wall word *hands* (holding up word card). *House* and *hands* sound the same at the beginning. I can use the word *hands* to help me write the word *house* because they both start with the same sound—/h/. Since the word I know—*hands*—begins with the letter *h, house* must also begin with the letter *h.*

D. Write the letter. (If appropriate, continue to orally segment the word, relating sounds to letters and referring to the ABC Wall for help in recording letters.)

(I model writing the letter *h* on chart paper, referring to the key word card. Depending on students' knowledge, I may continue.)

Teacher: *H* is a good start. But if I just write *h,* does that look like the word *house?* No, it's just one letter. What other sounds do you hear in the word *house*? (We say and slowly stretch the word *house.*)

Students: /s/

Teacher: Yes, I hear /s/ in *house.* What other words do you know with the /s/ sound?

(I assist students in thinking of /s/

words. These words can be written on chart paper so students can use them as models for figuring out the letter corresponding to /s/. If a word representing /s/ is already on the ABC Wall, that reference is used.)

Teacher: Since we have *sun* on our ABC Wall (or, since we know these /s/ words), we can use what we know to figure out the letter we need for the /s/ sound. What letter do I need?

Students: *s*

Teacher: Where do you hear /s/ in the word *house*? This is important because I need to decide whether to put the letter *s* before or after the letter *h*. I may need to say *house* again slowly to hear if the /s/ is at the beginning or end. Try it yourself. What do you think?

(After wait-time, I blend the possible letter combinations /h/—/s/ and /s/—/h/ to demonstrate the importance of letter placement. The class decides which placement of *s* works best.)

E. Evaluate the spelling attempt.

Teacher: Yes, *s* goes after the *h*. I hear /h/ at the beginning of the word *house* and /s/ at the end.

(I write *s* on the chart, referring to the key word *sun*.)

F. Continue thinking aloud and adding to the piece.

I continue to draft the story, stopping to model and engage students in segmenting a few words with key sounds. Before moving to independent writing time, we debrief about the lesson. The question, "What did you see me do as a writer?" involves students in explicit talk about strategy use. Responses may include:

"You thought about something that happened to you for a story idea."

"You said the words very slowly."

"You listened for sounds in the words you were trying to write."

"You used the ABC Wall to help you figure out what letters you need-ed."

We talk about how these same strategies are helpful to them as writers. Students are given plenty of opportunities to approximate and refine these behaviors during daily writing.

Things to Remember

- I model segmenting words and associating sounds with letters in purposeful ways every day. These lessons do not occur by chance. I *plan* to demonstrate, review, and explicitly talk about strategy use. This is how students learn *when, why,* and *how* to use their growing knowledge of letters and sounds.

- Students need to feel comfortable experimenting with communicating on paper. Using a brief mini-lesson, I demonstrate how writing changes developmentally. I show the class how beginners may scribble, make letter-like forms, and use random letters to write. Then, I demonstrate how pictures and beginning letters can be used to represent what students wish to communicate. I encourage students to write in a way that works for them and assure them their attempts will be accepted even though their writing may not look like writing in "real books." Students need to understand that we will work together *toward* more sophisticated ways to get our ideas on paper. The demonstrations are designed to move them toward this goal.

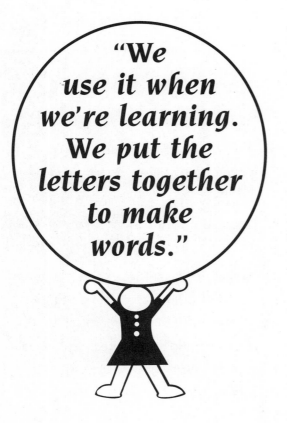

"We use it when we're learning. We put the letters together to make words."

Meeting Individual Needs

Using Word Walls to teach depends on careful consideration of students' needs and abilities. If students are just starting to write beginning letters for words, supporting their efforts to write *h* for *house* and the beginning letters of a few other words may be sufficient. As their ability to hear and represent initial letters improves, modeling should move to recording final letters (as in *s* for *house*), then medial letters. Once this point is reached, students will benefit from chunking (see Chapter 2). Of course, this technique works well with small groups of students and can be suited to their specific needs.

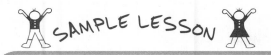

Using the ABC Wall During Reading

The following demonstration, using the text of a morning message (Routman, 1991), is designed to help emergent readers learn strategies for figuring out unknown words while reading. Among other strategies, we make analogies using words we know from the ABC Wall to decode initial sounds in new words.

Our daily message routine involves both a meaning focus and a print focus. We give the reading "a try," problem solve and discuss strategies as we go, discuss the message content, then focus on aspects of the print. In kindergarten and first grade, we circle initial and final letters, capitals and simple two and three letter chunks. This works the same in second and third grades, with focus on more sophisticated concepts such as hyphens and synonyms. We may also use the morning message as a source for Word Wall words.

Note: This demonstration lesson was done during a week in which the letter *l* was one focus.

The Morning Message contains meaningful information. Here, students are motivated to find out what's happening in class today.

What Is a Morning Message?

Everyday before class, I write a meaningful message on a portable, freestanding chalkboard. Students filter in and check the message, working with a friend or two, to find out what is happening. The message motivates them to read independently, since it relates to their day. I closely observe their independent reading to gain useful information about their use of cues. Often, we discuss their processes. I make observations and ask questions.

- "While you were giving the message a try, I noticed . . . ."
- "Why did you . . . ?"
- "What were you thinking when . . . ?"
- "How did you figure out . . . ?"

The Morning Message is a nice segue into independent message writing activities. Students often use the backside of the board to write their own messages to the class. Also, we have a message center, where students can post messages and compose mail for classmates.

The beauty of the morning message is that it only takes a few minutes, yet so much can be gained from this simple interaction. Students learn about the function of writing, concepts of print, the alphabetic principle, using the cueing systems, reading and spelling high-frequency words, and language form and mechanics.

 SAMPLE LESSON

Using the ABC Wall During Reading (Lesson Routine)

A. Write a message that is meaningful to students (or use another shared reading context). Allow students to "give it a try" by reading the message independently.

B. Read the message together. Stop to problem solve, referring to the Word Wall when appropriate.

C. Reread to check meaning.

A. Write a message that is meaningful to students.

Morning Message

Dear boys and girls,
We will go to gym.
We will take our books
to the library.

Love,
Mrs. Wag

> "If you don't know how to write a word, you can look up to find a word that sounds the same."

B. Read the message together.

Teacher: Everyone come to the rug to read this morning's message.

(Students come forward and attempt to read the message independently.)

Teacher: Now that everyone has given it a try, let's read it together.

Teacher & Students (reading chorally): "Dear boys and girls, We will go to gym. We will take our books to the . . ." (I stop reading.)

Teacher: That is a big word. What would fit there? What would make sense? We will take our books to the . . .

Students: Reading corner? Library?

Teacher: Yes, both *reading corner* and *library* make sense. Let's look at the first letter of the word. Do we know any other words that begin this way? (pointing to the letter *l*)

Student: Lion, like Leo the Lion.

Teacher: Yes, *lion* is the word on our ABC Wall for the letter *l*. What sound do you hear at the beginning of the word *lllllion*?

Students: /l/.

Teacher: So, if this word starts with /l/ like *lion*, it must be . . . ?

Students: Library!

C. Reread to check meaning.

Teacher: Yes, *lllllibrary*. It couldn't be *reading corner* because that doesn't begin with /l/. Let's read the sentence again to make sure *library* makes sense.

Teacher & Students: We will take our books to the library. Love, Mrs. Wag.

Teacher: Thanks for reading with me. *Library* does make sense and it begins with the letter *l* like our ABC Wall word *lion*. Good job figuring it out!

Sometimes, especially early in the year, there may not be a Word Wall word with an analogous beginning to help students figure out an unknown word. When this happens, I provide words by writing a few on the chalkboard. The best words are those students know, such as names. Read the words with the students and ask, "What do you notice about the way these words begin?" Then, relate the beginning sound to the unknown word in the text you are reading. This way, students can still be encouraged to use analogy regardless of the absence of a key word on the ABC Wall.

Things to Remember

- When writing morning messages for emergent readers, make the text supportive by using a repetitive structure. The text in the example, with the repetitive phrase "We will," becomes familiar to students when used daily. Additionally, picture cues may take the place of some words. This will give students more success in their independent reading attempts, and may also encourage them to use drawing in their own writing. As reading skills increase, the patterned structure is altered or dropped, picture cues become less frequent, and the morning message can be lengthened, providing more opportunities for discussion of strategy use.

- During shared reading with emergent readers, my voice may lead, with students reading just behind. This allows me to stop and strategize with students on any given word. One way students learn what readers do is by watching a model. I model frequently, thinking aloud about using the Word Wall as a reference.

- Sometimes teachers encourage strategy use in the morning message by leaving a few spaces blank. Students try to fill in each blank with a word that fits and makes sense. Other teachers make a few mistakes in the message to invite strategy talk as corrections are made.

● Another way to encourage strategy talk is to allow students to give the reading "a try" and report about their own problem solving. During a recent reading of the morning message, one of my students reported, "I see *p* like in *pail*" at the beginning of the word *paint*. The sentence read, "In art, we will paint." This sparked a discussion:

Teacher: How does knowing the word *pail* help you figure out this word?

Students: It starts with the same letter.

Teacher: So, if you know *pail,* (orally stretching and segmenting the word) /p/ . . . ail, you know the beginning sound is /p/. What else will help here?

Students: Think of what makes sense.

Teacher: Yes, (rereading from the morning message) 'In art, we will /p/. . .' What makes sense here?

Students: Paint!

Teacher: So, using what you know helps you figure out what you don't know. That's why we build and use our ABC Wall.

More Ways to Use the ABC Wall

● **Interactive Writing:** While sharing the pen with students, orally segment words and connect the sounds to known words on the ABC Wall. Allow students to write as much of the word as they can. Then, take the pen to complete the word or fill in unknown word parts.

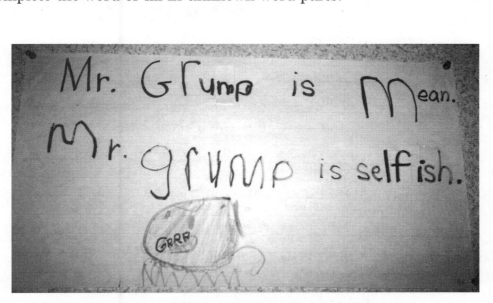

Response to shared reading of the Big Book <u>Mr. Grump</u> *(Wright Group).*

Kindergarteners and teacher share the pen to record the Daily News.

- **Recording the Daily News:** While recording the daily news, think aloud to model how to use the ABC Wall to write words. Encourage students to call out letters and sounds, or share the pen.

- **Writing Workshop:** Encourage students to make independent approximations using the ABC Wall. Assist students just as you would model aloud, helping them segment words and make analogies to known words. With beginners, I often share the pen right at their seats. They record initial letters (or as much as they can). Then I take the pen and fill in missingparts.

- **Reading Workshop:** Students use oversized pointers to "read the room" during reading workshop. They also use word frames, windows, or other devices to highlight known letters and words in their reading.

- **Reading Aloud:** Use an oral cloze procedure. As you read, pause on a word voicing only the beginning sound. This allows students to determine what makes sense and has that initial sound. Follow up with, "Yes the word is _____. It begins like our ABC Wall word _____."

- **Shared Reading:** Mask all but the beginning letters in a few words during shared reading to encourage making analogies to ABC Wall words.

- **Guided Reading:** Assist students in decoding an unknown word by covering all but the initial letter and referring them to a known word on the ABC Wall. If a matching key word is not on the ABC Wall, provide one or two (i.e., "This word starts like *tub* and *toe*").

- **Think Alouds:** Think aloud about how to use beginning sounds and the ABC Wall while writing on the chalkboard or in your journal. Think aloud about decoding using beginning sounds and the ABC Wall while reading with students.

- **Strategy Talk:** Debrief about strategy use when you finish a reading or writing

Teaching Reading & Writing with Word Walls • Scholastic Professional Books

session with questions such as, "What did we do to figure out this word?" and "What helped us to spell this word?" Ask students when they will use these strategies in the future.

REMEMBER: Anytime you read and write is an appropriate time to refer to and model use of the ABC Wall.

Classroom Snapshots
The ABC Wall Throughout the Year

BEGINNING OF YEAR

Building the ABC Wall is a process that takes time. This does not mean children are not learning other things about literacy and about other letters and sounds. Modeling the use of letter-sound cues is appropriately embedded in a variety of daily literacy activities. Additionally,

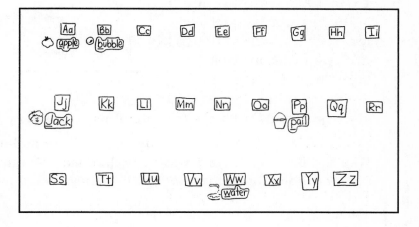

it is not just the number of words on the ABC Wall that matters; rather, children are learning a *strategy*—using words they *know* to read and write words they do not know.

MID-YEAR

You may set a goal for where you want your ABC Wall to be by mid-year. In the past, my kindergarten goal has been to have the alphabet covered by the end of the third quarter so we may begin building a simple Chunking Wall (see Chapter 2). Of course, the pace you sustain depends on the needs and abilities of your students, so the number of words on your ABC Wall by mid-year will vary. Regardless of the number of words, you may move on to the Chunking Wall and continue to add periodically to the ABC Wall, if appropriate.

END OF YEAR

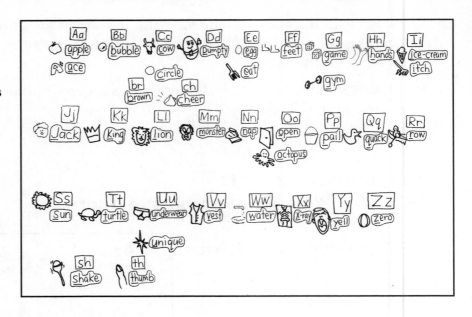

As the school year comes to a close, you may use the ABC Wall as an assessment tool. Students may be asked to complete a modified writing spree (Clay, 1979; 1993b), writing all of the key words or letters they know from the ABC Wall without looking. They may also be prompted to use these key words and/or letters to write other words they know.

Students leaving your class may benefit from making their own version of the ABC Wall to take with them for future reference. Manila file folders can be used to produce durable, individual ABC Walls—they even stand up!

FINAL THOUGHTS

Building and using an ABC Wall helps beginners learn and apply their knowledge of letters and sound–letter correspondences in reading and writing. Consider how the techniques described here help teachers meet the following recommendation made by the Committee on the Prevention of Reading Difficulties in Young Children (1998):

"The ABC Wall helps us learn the ABCs."

Kindergarten instruction should be designed to provide practice with the sound structure of words, the recognition and production of letters, knowledge about print concepts, and familiarity with the basic purposes and mechanisms of reading and writing. (Snow, Burns & Griffin, Eds., p. 322)

CHAPTER TWO

The Chunking Wall

> " I chunk, therefore I am. "

The Chunking Wall is made up of key words containing common spelling patterns, or chunks. These chunks, such as *-ake* in *cake* and *-art* in *dart*, help students read and write unknown words by analogy to known words rather than sounding out letter by letter or using phonetic rules. For example, using the key word *cake*, students may use analogy to read or write words such as *rake*, *bake*, and *snowflake*. The analogy strategy has proven effective in promoting word recognition and spelling abilities for developing readers and writers and has gained favor in the field of literacy (Brown, Sinatra, & Wagstaff, 1996; Cunningham, 1995; Fry, 1998; Gaskins, 1998; Gaskins, Ehri, Cress, O'Hara & Donnelly, 1997; Gaskins, Gaskins & Gaskins, 1991, 1992; Moustafa, 1997; Routman, 1996a; Strickland, 1998; Vacca, Vacca & Gove, 1995; Wagstaff, 1994; Wagstaff & Sinatra, 1995).

GETTING STARTED

Purposes of the Chunking Wall

I've used the Chunking Wall in the primary grades to:

- promote students' phonemic awareness
- teach students to look at words flexibly (i.e, look at onsets and rimes, prefixes and suffixes, or other familiar word parts, rather than letter by letter)
- help students decode unknown words by analogy
- help students spell words through analogy

The primary goal of the Chunking Wall is to help students read and spell unknown words quickly and efficiently using analogies. Decoding (reading words) and encoding (spelling words) by analogy have helped my students to increase their reading abilities as shown on informal reading inventories and to become more sophisticated and conventional spellers (Wagstaff, 1994).

The Chunking Wall is built with developing readers and writers who already have knowledge of letter names and basic letter–sound correspondences. This is not to say that students must know all letters and letter–sound correspondences before beginning a Chunking Wall. Such basic knowledge can be picked up as the Wall is built and used. Other reading and writing activities also contribute to this knowledge, but a phonetic base is certainly needed before students' attention is focused on word chunks.

My first experiences with "chunking" occurred in my second grade classroom. I noticed some students struggling to decode and spell words in a letter-by-letter fashion or by applying rules. Others were inefficient in their use of letter-sound knowledge. Even though they knew most letter–sound correspondences, their decoding was labored because they were still blending sound by sound instead of using larger word chunks to decode more efficiently. Also, phonetic rules were hard to remember and apply and had many exceptions. It seemed my instruction was not meeting my students' needs.

I knew there had to be a better way. I had read about the efficiency of using analogies, citing research that showed how chunks are stable units, easier to identify and use than individual phonemes. I recall thinking, "This could really be it!" Focusing more attention on onsets and rimes rather than individual letters made a great deal of sense to me. And, I quickly found, it made a great deal of sense to my second grade students too!

The analogy strategy complemented my meaning-focused approach. I was already teaching and modeling many reading strategies including previewing, predicting, using context clues, reading on, rereading, summarizing, and self-questioning. Using chunks to decode and spell new words added a strategy that helped students make the most of graphophonic cues.

As a reading specialist in a K–6 school, I worked with teachers school-wide to infuse the strategy into their language arts programs. The primary grade students benefited, as did struggling readers in intermediate grades. I continue to teach and model chunking because it works!

Building the Chunking Wall

While words on the ABC Wall are chosen for beginning sounds, key words for the Chunking Wall are chosen based on the utility of their chunks. I begin by focusing students' attention on onsets and rimes. A *rime* is the vowel and what comes after it in a syllable (i.e., *-ake* in *cake, -en* in *then*). An *onset* is the consonant or consonant cluster that comes before the vowel in a syllable (i.e., *c* in *cake, th* in *then, fl* in *flat*). Syllables might not have an onset (i.e., *it* and *at*), but they always contain a rime.

A chunk (rime) is useful if it is contained in many words. For example, *-en* is a useful chunk, because it appears in lots of words—*pen, then, tenant,* and *entrance.* On the other hand, generating a list of *-esk* words is not so easy. Thus, a key word containing *-esk* would not be chosen for the Chunking Wall because it is a less common chunk and thereby less useful to developing readers and writers. Key words may be one syllable or multisyllabic, but only one chunk is highlighted in each word. With emergent readers and writers, one-syllable words are often chosen as key words because they appear most frequently in beginning reading materials.

My students and I have had great success choosing key words for our Chunking Wall from poetry (Wagstaff, 1994). We enjoy the humorous nature of Shel Silverstein and Jack Prelutsky. Poetic rhyme and rhythm seem to help students remember key words. The use of poetry allows reinforcement of phonemic awareness, such as the ability to identify and generate rhyming words. Once a literature context such as a poem

What is an onset?

- consonant(s) before the vowel(s) in a syllable (*s* in *sit; spl* in *split*)
- not all syllables have an onset

What is a rime?

- the vowel(s) and what comes after in a syllable (*-it* in *sit; -oat* in *float*)
- all syllables have a rime
- also known as spelling patterns, phonograms, or chunks

is established through shared reading or writing, I choose with my students appropriate key words for practice and, ultimately, inclusion on the Chunking Wall. They determine if a word has a useful chunk. For example, if students choose the word *trick*, I ask, "Can you think of many *-ick* words?" Students offer analogous words orally such as *stick, picking,* and *licked.* If we generate many words, we decide the word will be helpful, and it is written on a card with the

Beginners and second language learners benefit from extra picture–cue support, which this simple chunking wall provides.

rime *-ick* underlined. If few words can be generated, we decide the chunk is infrequent and another word is chosen. Words may be chosen on Monday, their chunks practiced and reviewed throughout the week, then word cards containing each word are added to the Chunking Wall on Friday. Picture cues may accompany Chunking Wall words to lend secondary support to beginners and second language learners. The Chunking Wall is configured in *a, e, i, o, u* order according to the first vowel in the rime.

Other Types of Chunks

Prefixes, suffixes, and other common word parts such as *-tion* in *lotion* and *-le* in *apple* may be considered chunks. It is extremely helpful to point out various types of word chunks to students. This teaches them to look at words in many ways, enabling them to be flexible in applying the analogy strategy. We add key words with chunks other than rimes to the Chunking Wall under the heading "Other."

How many words should be added to the Wall each week?

The number of words chosen for the Chunking Wall varies depending on students' needs and abilities. Since skilled reading is fluent and automatic (Anderson, Hiebert, Scott, & Wilkinson, 1985), one goal of building and using a Chunking Wall is to help students develop automaticity in recognizing and spelling common chunks. In working toward this goal, selected chunks should be very familiar by the end of a week's lessons. This task is harder with more key words. Likewise, lessons for selecting words and wordplay activities are lengthened as the number of words for the week grows. I have found that, as a rule, two or three words each week may be ample for kindergarten and first grade, while five or more may work for second and third grades.

The number of words on the Chunking Wall is important because developing automaticity with as many chunks as possible will increase access to words during reading and writing. The ability to use chunks strategically is equally important. If students are unable to use learned chunks to generate spellings and decode unknown words by analogy, they have only expanded the number of sight words stored in their memories.

> **"The best differentiator between good and poor readers is repeatedly found to be their knowledge of spelling patterns and their proficiency with spelling-sound translations."**
>
> —Adams, 1990, p. 290

Meeting Individual Needs

There are many ways to introduce a new favorite. Reading aloud is one method; another is to start with a shared reading. Still another is to give students a copy of the material to be read and allow them to read silently, with partners, or in small groups before a shared reading occurs. I suggest using the read-aloud method most frequently at the beginning of the school year as a means of lending extra support to students. After children build more skills, get into the routine, and anticipate a new poem each week, they may attempt the first reading independently from a chart or overhead.

BEGINNING OF WEEK

SAMPLE LESSON

Adding to the Chunking Wall (Lesson Routine)

A. Read aloud and discuss a poem, rhyme, chant, or Big Book.

B. Choose key words and identify the chunks. Test the utility of each chunk by orally generating analogous words.

C. Write chosen key words on colored cards for the Chunking Wall, underlining the chunks.

D. Revisit the poem or book through rereading, dramatization, or innovating on the text.

A Tree Can Be . . .

by Judy Nayer

A tree can be . . .
a place to play,
a place to rest,
a place to hide,
and a place to nest.

A tree can be . . .
a place to swing,
a place to fly,
a place to climb,
and a place to stay dry.

A tree can be . . .
a place full of food,
a place full of sound,
a place full of life,
and it changes year-round.

A. Read aloud and discuss a poem, rhyme, chant, or Big Book.

I introduce a new poem, or *New Favorite* as we call it, at the beginning of the week by showing the title and/or cover illustration. Students make predictions about the poem's subject based on these clues and discuss them with peers. After sharing our ideas, I read aloud the poem and we check our predictions. We describe the visual images we formed as the poem was read and decide on the overall meaning of the piece. Often I reread the poem several times during our initial discussions to build familiarity. Then we may focus on print, reading the poem from a large chart, overhead, or photocopy.

In all lessons, we choose Chunking Wall words only after we have enjoyed the poem several times. This keeps the focus on the meaning of the whole rather than on individual words. When it is time to choose words, I may have a few in mind and allow students to pick additional words. Each word is tested for the utility of its chunk. If the chunk can be used to generate many words that we read and write, we know it will be a useful addition to our Chunking Wall.

Teacher: You gave our new favorite a good try. Would anyone like to comment on how the reading went?

Student: It was easy to read because it had so many of the same words.

Teacher: Will you show us where you noticed repeated words? (Student points and reads from poster.) Who else noticed how the words repeated? How did that help you to be a successful reader?

Student: If you figure out the words once, and you see them again, you don't have to figure them out again, you just read them.

Teacher: So noticing the pattern, or what words or phrases repeat in a poem or story, makes the reading easier. Who would like to share a word they had to figure out?

Student: I stopped the first time it said *place.*

Teacher: What did you do?

Student: Well, I noticed it looked like *face,* so I tried *pl-ace* and it worked.

Teacher: You noticed the *-ace* chunk? So you thought, 'If I know *face,* this must be *place.*' When you tried *place*—'A tree can be a *place* to swing'—it made sense. Then, once you figured out the word was *place,* you knew it right away when you saw it again on the next line.

Let's go ahead and read together. See what else you notice about how the author wrote the poem.

(Class reads the poem chorally. We continue to discuss aspects of the poem such as other repeated words, rhyme, and content.)

B. Choose key words and identify the chunks. Test the utility of each chunk by orally generating analogous words.

Teacher: Let's read the poem one more time. This time watch for words that might be good to add to our Chunking Wall. (After re-reading) Who sees a word with a good chunk that is not already on the Wall?

Student: *Nest.*

Teacher: What is the chunk in *nest*?

Students: *-est*

Teacher: Can you think of other words

with the -est chunk?

Students: *Rest, best, west, zesty, dressed...*

Teacher: Yes, dressed has the /est/ sound, but a different spelling pattern. How about *established*?

(Note that even though the proper syllable break in this word is after -es, the -est chunk may still be used in decoding and spelling it.)

C. Write chosen key words on colored cards for the Chunking Wall, underlining the chunks.

Teacher: Sounds like quite a few words. *Est* will probably be a useful chunk for our Chunking Wall. I'll write the key word *nest* on a card and underline the -est chunk. What other words have useful chunks?

Student: *Food.*

Teacher: What is the chunk in *food*?

Students: *-ood*

Teacher: Can you think of other *-ood* words?

Students: *Mood, poodle, rude, sued, noodle, viewed...*

Teacher: You've thought of many *-ood* words. Words that sound like -ood have more than one spelling, so later we will add other Chunking Wall words to help

us remember the different spellings. Right now, though, we can write *food* on a card for our Chunking Wall, underlining the -ood spelling pattern. Any other words?

Student: *Sound.*

Teacher: What chunk do you hear?

Students: *-ound*

Teacher: Can you think of other *ound* words? Words that rhyme with *sound*?

Students: *Pound, hound, mound, found, playground....*

Teacher: -Ound sounds like another useful chunk. How about *flounder*?

(I write *sound* on a card, underlining -ound.)

D. Revisit the poem or book through rereading, dramatization, or innovating the text.

Teacher: Now, here are the new Chunking Wall words we'll play with this week. Let's put them back into the poem and read it once more.

(Students match word cards to the poster, affixing them with sticky-tack. You may choose to read "A Tree Can Be . . ." during reading workshop and use the word cards and magnetic letters to write other words with these chunks.)

Things to Remember

- After students' first independent reading attempt, we begin the lesson by talking about their process. Encouraging talk about what went well and what was problematic sets the stage for sharing strategies. The dialogue here allows us to review the importance of text structure (in this case, repetitive, patterned text) and using chunks and analogy as a decoding strategy. If we want our students to be strategic readers and writers, strategy talk must be a component of daily literacy lessons.

- When choosing chunks for the Chunking Wall, teachers wonder about variability in spelling and sound. Some chunks have more than one spelling, as in the case of -ood, and some have more than one sound (as with ow—h<u>ow</u>/sh<u>ow</u>). This should not be cause for alarm, rather an opportunity to teach students to use strategies flexibly. In this lesson, the variability in spelling is simply mentioned. This is because I plan to follow-up with daily wordplay, at which time I can address variations in spelling or sound. To eliminate any remaining confusion, key words with an alternate spelling or sound are added to the Chunking Wall over time.

- Vocabulary and decoding teaching points often occur during the first readings. For example, during the first reading of "Spaghetti," a poem by Shel Silverstein, Jeff, a second grader, reported having difficulty reading the word *confetti*. Asked what he did to deal with this problem, he reported, "Well, I didn't know what it was at first, so I read on and I saw the word *spaghetti*. *Spaghetti* looks like *confetti* 'cause it has *-etti*. So, I knew it was *confetti*." We then had a discussion about the meaning of *confetti*.

Meeting Individual Needs

The difficulty of the lesson may be increased or decreased by selecting a more or less challenging poem. Shorter poems, rhymes, or chants with familiar content may be used to decrease lesson difficulty. After building ABC Walls in kindergarten and first grade, continued use of nursery rhymes and common chants is appropriate for work with chunks.

"Chunks are like -ot in pot and -ing in sing."

MID-WEEK PRACTICE ACTIVITIES

The following wordplay activities lend themselves to whole or small group situations involving teacher direction or as part of learning centers. I often choose an appropriate activity to follow-up my work with guided reading groups.

● **Chant and Check:** (Downer & Gaskins, 1986) This is an easy way to review the week's chunks. I hold up each key word card in turn. Students write the word on scratch paper, chant the word, and check the spelling. The group brainstorms two or three other words with the same chunk. As each word is offered, students spell it on their papers. Attempted spellings are written on the board or overhead and checked for accuracy. I always reinforce the strategy, "Yes, if this is *sound* (holding up the word card), s-o-u-n-d, with the *-ound* chunk, we must spell *ground*, g-r-o-u-n-d."

● **Word Ladders:** (Fountas and Pinnell, 1996) Have students start with a key word such as *nest*. Using the chunks in the key word, students generate a list of other related words. For example, "I know how to spell the word *nest*. *Rest* has the same chunk as *nest* (students write *rest*). *Rest* makes me think of *pest* (students write *pest*). In the word *pest*, I can remove a letter to make the word *pet* (students write *pet*). If I know how to spell *pet*, I can spell *let* (students write *let*). *Let* is part of the word *letter* . . ." Students can generate word ladders such as these independently or cooperatively.

"**I** see de *like he and* ous *like fabulous, so this word must be delicious.*"

● **Making Words:** (Cunningham, 1995) This activity builds spelling and decoding skills. Students manipulate letter cards to create words as directed by the teacher. They begin by making small words (i.e., three letter words such as *sat*), then bigger and bigger words until all cards are used to make one big word. As words are made, they are recorded on cards for future sorting.

- **Take Home Making Words:** (Cunningham, 1995) Students may take home a sheet like the one in Figure 9. After cutting apart the letters, the cards are manipulated to make words. Words are written in the spaces provided. These can be cut apart and sorted. Students can list their word sorts on another sheet of paper and share them with peers the next day.

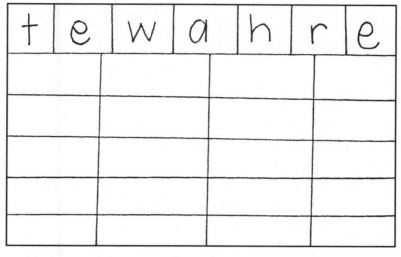

figure 9

- **Modified Take Home Making Words:** List the word chunks covered that week at the top of the take home sheet as pictured in Figure 10. Students cut apart the chunks and add their own beginning or ending letters to make new words. These words are listed in the spaces provided, cut apart, and sorted. Challenge kids to make words with chunks in the beginning, middle, *and* end. Who can come up with the longest or most unusual word?

ay	ill	ip	at

figure 10

- **Word Hunts:** Using the week's key words, direct students to hunt for words with analogous chunks and add them to classroom charts. (See Figure 11.) Challenge students to look for words containing those chunks in the beginning, middle, and end. As the charts are filled, they may be reviewed. Students may also add words to their spelling dictionaries.

- **Word Sorts:** On index cards, write words with chunks from the week's key words. Place the word cards in a sorting center. Challenge students to sort the words in any way they choose (i.e., by prefix, suffix, chunk, beginning letter, number of letters, or meaning).

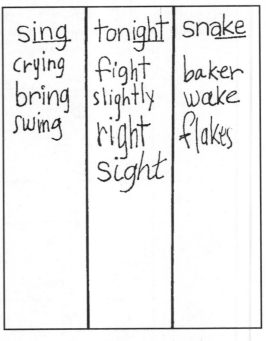

sing	tonight	snake
crying	fight	baker
bring	slightly	wake
swing	right	flakes
	sight	

figure 11

- **Magnet Boards:** Students make key words and words with the same chunk on magnet boards, mix the letters, and reform the words.

- **Push the Sounds:** Students "push the sounds" in words they make on the magnet board. Starting with the word at the bottom of the board, I model segmenting the word, taking the onset and pushing it upward while voicing the sound the letter stands for. Then, I push the rime upward, voicing its sounds. Students follow my lead. Once the word is reformed, we blend the sounds, running our fingers underneath while reading the word. We repeat this process several times. We also push the sounds at the phoneme level. This enables students to fully analyze the word, making it more accessible from memory (Gaskins, et. al, 1997).

- **Morning Message:** Students circle words with chunks from the Chunking Wall in the morning message.

- **Frame Words:** During shared reading, students frame words with chunks from the Chunking Wall.

- **Highlight Words:** Using pieces of transparent book cover, students highlight words with chunks from the Chunking Wall in print around the room.

- **Match Words:** Students match the key word cards to the shared reading poster during reading workshop.

● **Read the Room:** With a partner, students use special pointers to read and spell the words on the Chunking Wall as they "read the room."

● **Reread New Favorite:** Using an overhead projector, students reread copies of the new favorite and use magnetic letters to make words on the screen. Students keep copies of each week's new favorite in their favorites folders. They partner up or work in small groups to read and reread poems collected throughout the year. They gain fluency and confidence with these repeated readings, along with heightened awareness of Word Wall words. Groups often perform a reader's theater or poetic mini-drama for the class. We share our favorites with parents two times a year, during our Fall and Spring Flings, when students read a piece of their original writing from writing workshop.

Students of all ages (here, second graders) love to read and reread "Favorites."

● **Individual Reading:** Students reread their personal copies of the poem individually, in small groups, and at home.

● **Sentence Strips:** Students reread the poem from sentence strips and/or word cards in a pocket chart. I cut apart key words by onset and rime or by letters. Students take the letters, words, or sentences, mix them, and reorder them, reciting the poem.

● **Practice Pages:** (Wagstaff, 1994) Students complete and reread practice pages. Practice pages associated with the Chunking Wall are designed to promote automaticity with chunks. I list the key words of the week on the left side, underlining each chunk. Together, the students and I generate analogous words with the same chunk. These are written underneath each key word. On the right side of the paper, I provide a sentence using the key word as a context clue. (See Figure 12.) Students fold the paper on the dotted line and practice reading the key word, chunk, and analogous words. If they need help, they turn the paper over for the context clue. Partners take turns being "the teacher" by pointing to the words and asking "the student" to read them.

figure 12

Practice pages accumulate throughout the year in our practice folders. We might read from our folders for a few minutes as a word study activity for the day. Practice sessions are very brief, lasting only four to five minutes. Students like to challenge themselves to see how many pages they can work through during the short time allotted. Practice folders may be taken home periodically, so students can show their growing knowledge of words and chunks.

Additional Resources

If you're looking for illustrated poems that may be copied for the class, look for poetry pages in *Instructor* and the following books:

Goldish, M. (1993). *Thematic Poems, Songs, and Fingerplays: 45 Irresistible Rhymes and Activities to Build Literacy.* New York: Scholastic, Inc.

   —(1994). *Animal Poems from A to Z: More Than 100 Rhymes and Related Activities.* New York: Scholastic, Inc.

   —(1996). *Science Poems and Songs for Young Learners.* New York: Scholastic, Inc.

   —Katz, B. (1996). *Poems Just for Us! 50 Read-Aloud Poems with Cross-Curricular Activities for Young Learners.* New York: Scholastic, Inc.

Liatsos, S. (1995). *Poems to Count On: 32 Terrific Poems and Activities to Help Teach Math Concepts.* New York: Scholastic, Inc.

Moore, H. (1997). *A Poem a Day: 180 Thematic Poems and Activities That Teach and Delight All Year Long.* New York: Scholastic.

Poetry Place Anthology. (1983). New York: Scholastic.

END OF WEEK

At the end of the week, the new key words are affixed to the Chunking Wall. Sometimes, we take a mini "spelling test" to reinforce the idea that knowing these chunks is important. Students like to challenge themselves to know the words on the Chunking Wall. During workshop or learning center time on Fridays, they occasionally choose to partner-up and test each other. Some students even include knowing the Word Wall words as part of their individual literacy goals recorded in portfolios!

Connecting the Chunking Wall to Reading and Writing

After beginning the Chunking Wall, I show my students how to use the words on the Wall when reading and writing. The following lessons demonstrate how I connect the Chunking Wall to authentic reading and writing experiences.

Using the Chunking Wall During Writing

Interactive writing, a daily component of reading recovery lessons (Clay, 1993; Pinnell & McCarrier, 1994), provides a perfect opportunity to demonstrate using chunks strategically in real writing contexts. The writing may be initiated in various ways, including a response to reading or experiences across curricular areas. I negotiate with students the text to be written. The pen is shared as students are prompted to write what they can, while I jump in to add difficult elements.

In the following example, the students and I engage in interactive writing as a response to a shared reading of *I Like the Rain* (Belanger, 1988). Together, we create a weather chart for future classroom use. During the lesson we review chunks from previous weeks.

Lesson Routine

A. Generate a topic based on reading or experiences.

B. Orally negotiate the text with students. Segment words to be written into chunks, then spell the words by using the Chunking Wall or other known words as references. Share the pen with students.

C. Read and reread as the text is written. Revisit the text often.

"*I know the chunks on the Wall. They help in my reading and writing.*"

A. Generate a topic based on reading or life experiences.

Teacher: Tell your neighbor what you think about *I Like the Rain*.

(Students share with each other. I may listen and choose comments to share or ask for volunteers to share.)

Student: I like how the kids do different things.

Teacher: Tell us more about that.

Student: They make snowmen in the snow and play on the beach in the summer.

Teacher: What would you say this book is about if you were to tell a friend about it? Think for a minute and tell your neighbor.

Students: It's a book about seasons.

Students: Different weather in different seasons.

Students: And what people do in different seasons, what they wear . . . because of the weather.

Teacher: Yes, *I Like the Rain* shows different types of weather and the kinds of things kids may like to do in different weather. Since the book shows different types of weather, we could use it to make our own weather chart to keep track of the weather we have. We could take time each day to observe the weather and record our findings. What do you think of that idea? Tell your neighbor a title you think might work for our chart. (Think, pair-share.) What are some of your ideas?

Students: Our weather chart.

Students: Weather.

Students: Kinds of weather.

Students: Weather watching.

B. Orally negotiate the text with students. Segment words to be written into chunks, then spell the words by using the Chunking Wall or other known words as references. Share the pen with students.

Teacher: Those are all good ideas for a title. They fit what we are going to write on our chart. Which title should we use? (Class cooperatively decides on a title.) Why do you think we like the title "Weather Watching?" Say it with me, *wwweather wwwatching.* What do you notice?

Students: They start with /w/.

Teacher: Yes, both words start with the same sound, so it is fun to say. Say it with me again, *wwweather wwwatching.* We know we need the letter *w* to start writing the word *weather* for our title because the letter *w* stands for /w/. Who would like to begin our chart? (Volunteer comes forward.) Where do we need to start writing the title? What kind of *w* do we need for the title? (As student begins . . .) Yes, we need to write the title at the top and begin with a capital letter because titles start with capitals. (Student finishes writing a capital *W* and returns the marker to the teacher.) So, we have the beginning of our word. What chunks do you hear in the word *weather*? Say it slowly, weath . . . er.

Students: /eath/, /ûr/.

Teacher: /eath/ is not a chunk you will hear very often. It has a funny spelling here. (I add e-a-t-h to the chart). But, you also heard a common chunk, /ûr/. What Chunking Wall word do we know with the /ûr/ chunk?

Students: Her.

Teacher: So, if we know *her,* how might you spell /ûr/ at the end of *weather*?

Students: E-r. (Volunteer comes forward and completes *weather.*)

Teacher: We know we need another *w* for the word *watching.* Again, we need a capital because it is part of the title and we need to remember to add a space between the words. Who will give it a try? (Volunteer adds *W.*) Now, what chunks do you hear in *watching*? Let's say it slowly and listen for the chunks. *Watch . . . ing.*

Students: /och/, /ing/.

Teacher: /och/ in this case is spelled like the chunk -*atch* in *hatch* and *batch*, even though it has a different sound. (I add *a-t-c-h.*) Mostly when you see *a-t-c-h* in words it will say /ach/ like in *match.* Maybe later we will add a word to the Chunking Wall to help us remember that chunk. But you heard a very common chunk at the end of *watching,* the /ing/ chunk. What word do you know that will help us write /ing/?

Students: Sing.

Teacher: *Sing* is on our Chunking Wall. So, if s-i-n-g is *sing*, how might we spell /ing/ in *watching*? (Volunteer adds i-n-g to complete *watching*.) Now we have our title, (pointing) 'Weather Watching.' Let's list the kinds of weather we will watch for. What types of weather do you remember seeing in the book?

Students: Rain, sun, snow, wind . . .

Teacher: Which should we write first?

Student: Let's start with rain.

Teacher: How might you begin to spell *rain*? If we say it slowly we can hear the beginning sound and the chunk, *rrrrr . . . ain*. What do you hear?

Students: /r/, /ain/.

Teacher: What letter do we need to begin? (Volunteer adds *r* to the chart.) What was the chunk you heard in *rain*? Let's say it again slowly. *Rrr . . . aaaiiinnn.*

Students: /ain/.

Teacher: Yes, I hear /ain/. Do you know any words with the /ain/ chunk?

Students: *Plane, Jane, train* . . .

Teacher: *Train* and *Jane* are on our Chunking Wall and both have the /ain/ chunk. Which

Shared reading leads to shared writing across curricular areas. Here we "shared the pen" to create a weather chart after reading I Like the Rain *(Rigby).*

spelling do you think is correct for the /ain/ chunk in *rain*: *a-i-n* or *a-n-e*? Let's try them both on the chalkboard and see if we can tell. Good spellers often use chunks in words they know to spell other words. They also try different spellings for words they are unsure of, then check to see which spelling looks right. (Volunteers try *rain* with a-i-n and a-n-e. The group might also be asked to write *rain* both ways on scratch paper.) Which one looks right to you? Which have you seen before in your reading? Tell your neighbor what you think. (Students come to consensus about which spelling is correct. With more difficult words, small groups may use dictionaries to confirm spellings.)

Let's go ahead and finish *rain* on our chart. Someone also mentioned seeing *sun* in the book. Say the word *sun*. What do you hear at the beginning? What chunk do you hear?

Students: /s/, /un/.

Teacher: *Sun* is a pretty easy word. Who can write it for us? (Volunteer comes forward, takes the pen, and writes *sun*.) Yes, *sun*, s-u-n. The *-un* chunk is spelled u-n like in our Chunking Wall word *fun*.

C. Read and reread as the text is written. Revisit the text often.

The class continues this process, naming different types of weather. The writing may take place across several days. The text is then revisited for rereading.

Things to Remember

- First experiences with interactive writing take longer. In those cases, I sometimes take more of the responsibility for writing. As students become accustomed to sharing the pen and their knowledge of sound-spelling patterns grows, sessions proceed more quickly and more responsibility is taken by students. I have two options if students' attention begins to wane during interactive writing sessions. First, I may take control of the pen and finish the word or sentence, thinking aloud as I proceed. Second, I may stop the session in a logical place and make additions when the writing is revisited the following day.

- Teachers often ask how to handle student mistakes during interactive writing sessions. I want the text to be a positive model, so in most cases, if a mistake is made, we cover it with white correction tape. The student can then write the correction on the tape. We talk about how mistakes are common occurrences in the writing process. This is also discussed during modeled writing sessions.

- Interactive writing provides opportunities to model strategies as well as to review mechanics and concepts of print in context. Additionally, interactive writing helps children understand the writing process.

- Note how the spelling of the *-ain* chunk was handled in the lesson. Some chunks like this one have more than one spelling. Students learn to use analogy to generate multiple spellings and visually discriminate between attempts. Adults often use the same strategy. Also note how some words have chunks that are infrequent (as in the word w<u>ea</u>ther) or have more than one sound (as in the word w<u>atch</u>ing). Words like these should not be avoided. If students get stuck, I or a student volunteer may simply provide the spelling of these word parts.

- What if the Chunking Wall does not have a key word for a needed chunk? This often happens. I ask students to supply a word they know, or search the room or other references for analogous words. If students supply a word from memory but cannot spell it, I spell it for them on the board. This is then used to draw an analogy. Another way of dealing with this is to provide students with a few words and ask which would be helpful in spelling the unknown word. For example, the words *play, face,* and *pain* could be given for *rain.* Students could then identify *pain* as having the sounds and use that word to spell *rain.* Providing key words to choose from is a good strategy for lending more support to beginners or students who are having difficulty.

- Occasionally, if students are stuck on a word, Elkonin boxes (1973) may be used. They provide visual support for breaking a word apart orally and properly placing letter-sounds. Using the chalkboard, I draw one sound box for each sound in a word. As the word is said slowly, students fill in the boxes they can, focusing on the placement of letters (beginning, middle, or end), and I fill in the rest as needed. Once the word is fully analyzed and correctly spelled, a volunteer adds it to the interactive writing chart.

Meeting Individual Needs

More fluent readers and writers will need less teacher support and fewer references to the Chunking Wall, since more sound–spelling patterns and chunks will be stored in memory. The goal is, over time, to move students to this fluent, automatic stage.

Second and third graders may know how to spell the words recorded on the chart in this lesson. Therefore, time is not spent stretching the sounds in words, listening for chunks, and using the Chunking Wall or memory to find analogous words. The analogy strategy is only used to read and write unknown words. The texts generated during interactive writing sessions at these grade levels naturally have more multisyllabic words and complex sentence structures, so there are plenty of opportunities for using strategies and reviewing mechanics.

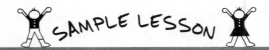

Using the Chunking Wall During Writing

The following writing lesson took place in a third grade classroom after a reading workshop focused on nonfiction. Students were reading a variety of texts complementing their study of extinct and endangered animals. Follow-up wordplay activities involved reading and writing new words using the key word *extinction*. The lesson demonstrates how reading can be the source of much word work.

Lesson Routine

A. Highlight a key word from any reading context. Analyze the chunks in the word and have students read a few new words containing a chunk (or chunks) from the key word.

B. Discuss strategies associated with decoding and determining meaning.

C. Have students write a few new words with the chunk (or chunks) in the key word.

D. Discuss strategies used when making spelling attempts.

A. Highlight a key word from any reading context. Analyze the chunks in the word and have students read a few new words containing a chunk (or chunks) in the key word.

Teacher: You know the word *ex-tinc-tion* from your reading. Use what you know about the chunks in extinction and other words to read these to your neighbor.

(I reveal the following words one-by-one on the overhead projector: *expire, flexing, Mexican food, Kleenex, hexagon.* As each word is revealed, students pair up to share. In each case, word meaning and strategies for decoding are briefly discussed.)

B. Discuss strategies associated with decoding and determining meaning.

Teacher: Talk to your neighbor about how you figured out this word (showing *hexagon*). Who would like to share a strategy with the class?

Student: I saw *ex,* so I knew *hex*, and *gon* was easy because of *on*.

Teacher: What about the meaning of the word?

Student: A six-sided shape.

Teacher: Yes, the chunk *hex* is a clue to meaning here. It is a Greek root meaning 'six'.

What do you notice about the *ex* chunk in these words (showing the list of *ex* words on the overhead)?

Students: *Ex* can be at the beginning, middle, or end of words.

C. Students write a few new words with the chunk (or chunks) in the key word.

Teacher: Let's try to write a few words with the *ex* chunk. Share some words that have *ex*. Think of words that have *ex* in different places, then, work with your neighbor to write those words.

(Students work cooperatively to generate a list of words with *ex*. I circulate, assisting problem solving and looking for examples to share with the class.)

Teacher: I noticed difficulty with the word *expel*. Try that word with your partner.

(Students try *expel*. I circulate, handing the pen to partners to write their attempt on the overhead. Students generate *exspell*, *exspelle*, and *expel*. As each pair writes their attempt, they are asked to explain how they arrived at that spelling.)

Student: It begins with *ex*, like *extinc-*

tion. Then we heard *spell*, as in *spelling.*

D. Discuss strategies used when making spelling attempts.

(After attempts are written and explained)

Teacher: Each of these is a good attempt. An editor would be able to easily figure out that you wrote *expel*. What could you do to find out which of these is the correct spelling?

Students: Ask an expert.

Students: Use a dictionary or spell-check.

Students: If you know the word is in a book or on a chart, you could find it.

Teacher: Those are good strategies. When you're not sure about a spelling, you can listen for the chunks, think of other words you know with those chunks, and try the spelling different ways like we did on the overhead. Then ask yourself, 'Which one looks right?' Let's try it.

(We look at each spelling, crossing out those that do not look right until the correct spelling is identified. To close the lesson, I debrief about strategies and add *extinction* to the Chunking Wall.)

Things to Remember

- A key word from any reading context may be used to illustrate the analogy strategy. Even without a Chunking Wall, students can learn to use known words to read and write new words.

- This type of lesson may follow guided reading sessions. Each group "reads a few and writes a few" words based on a chunk (or chunks) found in a key word from their reading.

Meeting Individual Needs

This lesson example emphasized one chunk—*ex*. Students "read a few and wrote a few" new *ex* words. However, open-ended wordplay allows flexibility for more skilled students. For example, after reading Jack Prelutsky's poem "A Pizza The Size of the Sun," students focused on three "power words": *delectable, massive,* and *resplendent*. After defining the words based on context, students were challenged to read new words containing *any* chunk from *any* of the three words (i.e., *aggressive, dentures, irritable*). Then they were asked to write a few new words containing *any* chunk from the key words. Partners spelled many new words using analogy.

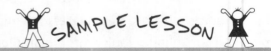

SAMPLE LESSON

Using the Chunking Wall During Reading

During shared reading, I often mask a few whole words or word parts to encourage use of structure, meaning, and graphophonic cues. Such lessons imitate coming to an unknown word during reading, allowing students to practice reading strategies in context. When we come to the covered word, we think about what would make sense and draw analogies to words on the Chunking Wall. We then cross check the chunks as the word is unmasked.

Lesson Routine

A. Mask a few words from a shared reading context.

B. Predict words that fit and make sense.

C. Cross check the first chunk, slowly unmasking it. If necessary, reread and make new predictions. Then cross check additional chunks.

D. Make analogies to Chunking Wall words.

E. Reread to check meaning and debrief about strategy use.

A. Mask a few words from a shared reading context.

The following exchange occurred in a second grade classroom while reading Janell Cannon's *Stellaluna*. I copied a page of the text onto an overhead, masking one challenging word (disappearing) with a self-sticking note. We read together from the overhead and paused when we came to the unknown word.

B. Predict words that fit and make sense.

Teacher: Her bat ways were quickly . . . What would fit here? What would make sense?

Students: Replaced.

Students: Changed.

Students: Forgotten.

Teacher: Great! Each of those words makes sense. We know from our reading that Stellaluna is becoming less and less like a bat and more like a bird. If you were really stuck on the unknown word, you could substitute one of those. They fit the overall context, or what's happening in the story. Let's check our predictions with the letters.

C. Cross-check the first chunk, slowly unmasking it. If necessary, reread and make new predictions. Then cross-check additional chunks.

(I unmask the first chunk, showing *dis*.)

Teacher: Based on the first chunk, could the word be *replaced, changed,* or *forgotten*?

Students: No. The right letters aren't there.

Teacher: Let's go back and reread, voicing the first chunk. What would make sense? "Her bat ways were quickly *dis . . .*"

Students: Dismissed.

Students: Discarded.

Teacher: Let's check the next chunk. (I unmask *-ap.*) Is it *dismissed* or *discarded*?

Students: No. It could be *disappearing*.

D. Make analogies to Chunking Wall words.

Teacher: Let's try it. "Her bat ways were quickly dis—ap—pear—ing." (I unmask each chunk as it is read.) *Disappearing* fits and makes sense. I see *-ear* like *hear* and *-ing* like *sing*, our Chunking Wall words. It must be *disappearing*! Tell your neighbor how we figured out the unknown word.

E. Reread to check meaning and debrief about strategy use.

Following a brief pair-share, I ask, "How did we figure out this word?" This way, our strategy use is explicitly described. Then, we continue reading.

Things to Remember

- Masking is one of my favorite techniques. It doesn't take a lot of time or preparation, it works with any text, and it sets up conditions for strategy use. Masking can occur in any shared reading context including a Big Book, text on an overhead, shared reading poster, or the morning message. To keep the focus on meaning, I am careful to only mask a few words for a planned reading session. When this technique is used daily, everyone benefits from countless opportunities for strategizing cooperatively.

- Sometimes when a word is masked, I record predictions on the chalkboard or overhead with student assistance. For example, I might ask, "If the word is *replaced,* what spelling pattern do you expect to see? What chunk do you hear at the beginning?" As students answer, chunk by chunk, the word is recorded and spellings are matched to key words on the Chunking Wall. Multiple predictions can be quickly chunked and spelled before unmasking the covered word.

- If students are unable to make a prediction based on what fits and makes sense for a covered word, unmask the first letter or first chunk. This usually provides enough support to get predictions flowing.

"I try to read the first letter (of an unknown word), then I go to the chunk."

Meeting Individual Needs

Masking can be varied to challenge and support different types of readers. When I am working with emergent readers, I might mask a word that is part of a repetitive phrase to help them notice and use text structure. More support is also present when only the rime in a word is covered (exposing the onset). Students learn to voice the beginning sound as they think about what fits and makes sense. Words that are predictable based on context are easier to figure out than those that are not. Support beginning readers by masking highly predictable words; challenge more advanced readers by masking less predictable multisyllabic words.

Teaching Reading & Writing with Word Walls • Scholastic Professional Books

More Ways to Use the Chunking Wall

Modeled Writing: Demonstrate chunking by thinking aloud while writing. I compose stories, poems, letters, or reports in front of students on chart paper. Completing a piece takes time. I return to the writing day after day during our opening mini-lesson for writing workshop. As I write, I think aloud about many composing strategies including spelling words by analogy using the Chunking Wall.

Examples of Modeled Writing

Recording the Daily News: Allow students to call out chunks and analogous words from the Chunking Wall to spell new words as the daily news is recorded.

For the daily news, I select one student to share a statement about an event in his life or anything else he wishes to share with the group. We discuss the statement. Then I record the news in front of the class on a large sheet of paper.

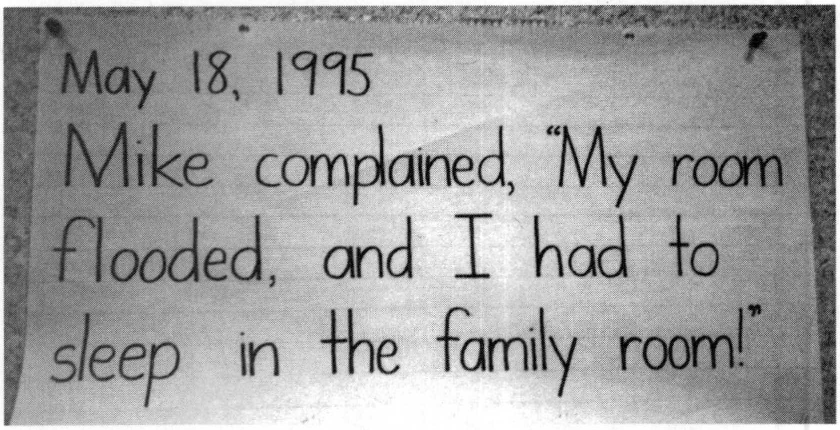

May 18, 1995
Mike complained, "My room flooded, and I had to sleep in the family room!"

Students "called out," helping the teacher record Mike's news.

Writing Workshop: Encourage students to spell unknown words by listening for the chunks and using key words from the Chunking Wall. Students become proficient at helping each other chunk and spell words. When the piece is turned in for editing, corrections are recorded above misspellings. During publishing, correct spellings may be recorded in individual spelling dictionaries.

Challenge Words: Occasionally, we open writing workshop with a review of spelling strategies. Students volunteer challenging words they might use that day in their writing. We pick a few to spell. Students listen for chunks and think of the spelling of other words they know to make logical attempts. These are recorded on the overhead or chalkboard so we can find the one that looks correct. (See Figure 13.) We discuss ways to confirm conventional spellings. As students proceed to independent writing time, they are reminded to use the spelling strategies we just practiced.

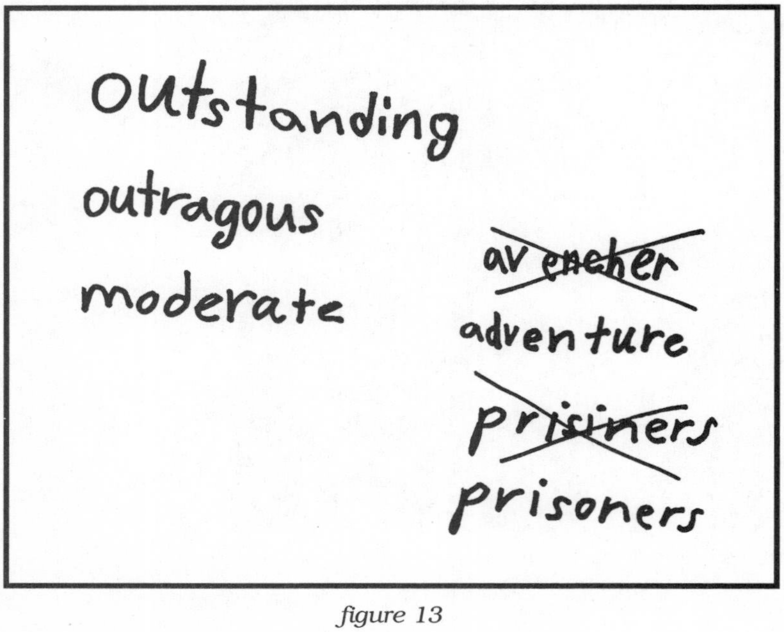

outstanding
outragous
moderate
av ~~encher~~
adventure
pr~~isiners~~
prisoners

figure 13

Have-a-Go (Routman, 1991): Twice weekly, starting in second grade, we devote approximately ten minutes to Have-a-Go spelling. Students look over their writing to identify words that "don't look right." Misspellings are recorded in the first column of the Have-a-Go sheet. In the second and third columns, students attempt the correct spelling. The final column is reserved for verifying the conventional spelling. I model the process several times to get it started. During Have-a-Go time, I circulate, discussing strategies and confirming correct spellings with individuals. We often relate spellings to words on the Chunking Wall or other known words.

HAVE A GO			
Try #1	Try #2		Correct Spelling
eskap	eskape		escape
rober	robber		robber
coud	cood	cude	could
greaty	greety		greedy

Shared Reading: Think aloud the use of analogies to decode words while reading with children. Simple observations like, "This word has the same chunk as our Chunking Wall word *bike*. It must be *hike*," take only a few seconds. Model using analogy for simple and multisyllabic words to reinforce the strategy at varied levels.

Reading Workshop: Students record difficult words from their reading on index cards, putting them in the *Big Word of the Day Box*. As the day ends, one big word is pulled from the box. The student comes forward and demonstrates how she figured out the word. Often, these demonstrations involve chunking.

Reading Aloud: Use oral cloze when reading aloud. As you read, pause on a few words voicing only the onset. Students naturally chime in. Respond to predictions with, "Could be. That fits and makes sense. Let me look at the chunks. I see, *-old* like *fold*, *-er* like *her*, and *-ing* like *sing*, it must be (everyone usually chimes in again given all these clues) *smoldering*!"

Guided Reading: Assist students in decoding an unknown word by using your finger or an index card to isolate the chunks. If needed, refer to the Chunking Wall. If a matching key word is not on the Chunking Wall, provide one or two (i.e., "This chunk is also in the words *hatch* and *match*").

Highlighting: Sometimes I hand out copies of a selected reading (a brief newspaper or magazine article, for example) so students can use highlighters to highlight chunks in words. I also write letters pertaining to the class, make copies, and encourage students to highlight useful chunks as they read.

Strategy Talk: Take time to debrief about strategy use. After modeling sessions, ask questions like, "What did you see me do as a writer?" or "What did you see me do as a reader?" to help students explicitly identify useful strategies. After shared reading and writing, get students talking about, "What we did to figure out this unknown word" or "What we did to spell this word." Encourage them to think about when they will use these strategies in the future.

REMEMBER: Anytime you read and write is an appropriate time to refer to and model use of the Chunking Wall.

Classroom Snapshots
The Chunking Wall Throughout the Year

BEGINNING OF YEAR

Some teachers begin the year focusing on the most frequent chunks as identified by researchers (Wylie & Durrell, 1970; Fry, 1998). In *The Reading Teacher* (1998, p. 61), Edward Fry identified 38 rimes which make up 654 different one-syllable words. They are listed in rank order according to frequency.

1. ay	2. ill	3. ip	4. at	5. am	6. ag
7. ack	8. ank	9. ick	10. ell	11. ot	12. ing
13. ap	14. unk	15. ail	16. ain	17. eed	18. y
19. out	20. ug	21. op	22. in	23. an	24. est
25. ink	26. ow	27. ew	28. ore	29. ed	30. ab
31. ob	32. ock	33. ake	34. ine	35. ight	36. im
37. uck	38. um				

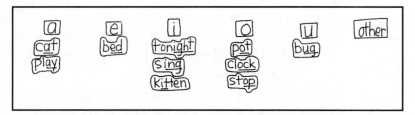

figure 14: A developing second grade wall in September.

MID-YEAR

As the Chunking Wall continues to grow, an "Other" category can be added for chunks and those nonrime, frequent chunks such as prefixes and suffixes.

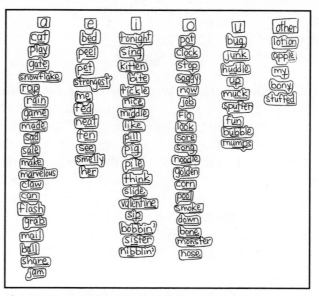

figure 15: Developing second grade wall in January

END OF YEAR

Some teachers prefer to stop adding to the Chunking Wall by mid-April, using the rest of the year to review and work on automaticity. Figure 16 represents a Chunking Wall with key words added throughout the whole school year.

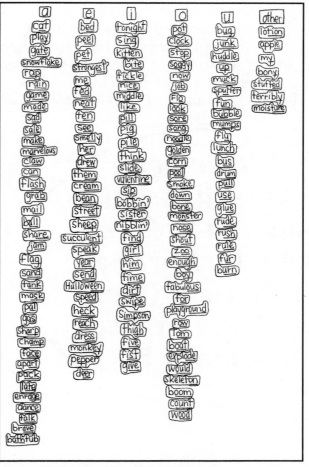

figure 16: The word wall in June

FINAL THOUGHTS

Be flexible when working with word chunks. Often, there is more than one way to break up a word. Recently, some colleagues were arguing over the correct way to chunk the word *candy*. They asked me, "What's the chunk, *and* or *an*?" I replied, "Does it matter? Either way, you come up with the correct word." We're not looking for perfect syllabication here, just a way to get to the word. I teach kids to look for the known part of the word—sometimes that's a rime, sometimes not; sometimes it's a chunk in the middle or at the end of the word. Frequently, students decode multisyllabic words by figuring out just one chunk combined with what makes sense in the sentence. This gives them enough information to read the whole word, cross-checking additional chunks.

I am often asked, "What do you do with high ability readers and writers?" My work in second grade convinced me that even students who were reading and writing above grade level benefited from the analogy strategy. Some of these kids were already "chunking" but at a subconscious level (as indicated by their subvocalizations, Wagstaff, 1994). Bringing the strategy to the conscious level helped them use it more purposefully and gave them increased confidence when reading and writing big words. But remember, don't teach strategies for sounding out words so students will always sound out words! We are trying to move students through developmental stages toward fluency. If you have students who are proficiently reading and writing multisyllabic words, let them read and write!

"When you try to spell a chunk, you can look up there. It shows you because it (the chunk) has a black line under it."

Lastly, starting to chunk with students does not mean you may never again mention individual letter-sounds. I often use analogy at this level, too, comparing a sound in one word to another. Additionally, when we "push the sounds" in words, we may work all the way through the phoneme level. Gaskins, et al. (1997) suggest this may aid students' ability to retrieve key words from memory.

CHAPTER THREE

The Words-We-Know Wall

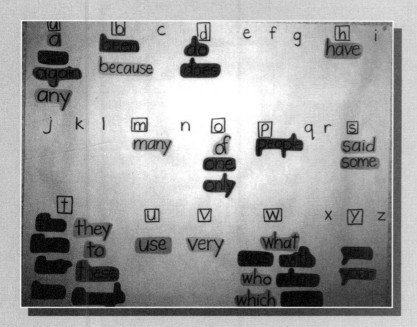

Spelling . . .

"what a topic
words on a page
and nothing more
(letters in the right places)

yet, so much
hearts and dreams
aches and themes
fashioned from lines and spaces

spelling . . .

words on a page
feed the form
feel the function
presentation counts!"

—J.W.

The Words-We-Know Wall contains high-frequency words that lack predictable spelling patterns, such as *the, said,* and *have.* These words are easy to find and can be harvested from any print source including rhymes, chants, and poems. In kindergarten, we often take words from the Morning Message. Students become familiar with these words, reading them day after day as part of the message. Another alternative is to use students' writings as a context for harvesting words. I often ask permission to copy student samples on the overhead. We notice how frequently specific words appear. We discuss the dangers of continually misspelling these words and make a commitment to work together on their conventional spellings. Additionally, as we grapple with spelling these high-frequency words during interactive and shared writing, we make additions to the Words-We-Know Wall.

The Words-We-Know Wall first came about based on the needs I saw in my second graders' writing. I was worried about those who repeatedly misspelled irregular high-frequency words, especially as the year progressed. Unlike other words that are spelled using invented spellings by developing spellers, these words are so frequent that mis-spelling them over and over may result in bad spelling habits. As a reading specialist working in a K-6 school, I was again reminded of the importance of this Word Wall while reviewing the writings of intermediate-level students. Although the content was more sophisticated, many older students were misspelling the same words that had given my second graders trouble. I was struck by how these misspellings neg-atively affected the overall impression of the piece. Yet many of these students were the same ones achieving top grades on Friday spelling tests.

I promote the Words-We-Know Wall for use at all grade levels. Look at your students' writing. Do many students frequently misspell words such as *they, have, what, does,* and *because*? If so, try building and using the Words-We-Know Wall. The idea is so simple; the results may surprise you!

> *"It is realistic to expect children—even young chil-dren—to spell basic high-frequency words correctly. Older children should be inventing only new vocab-ulary words, uncommon words, and words we wouldn't expect them to know how to spell."*
>
> —Routman, 1996, p. 51

GETTING STARTED

Purposes of the Words-We-Know Wall

I have used the Words-We-Know Wall to:

- help students accurately spell high-frequency words

- assist students in gaining automaticity in reading high-frequency words

I primarily build the Words-We-Know Wall as a spelling aid. The goal is for stu-dents to accurately and automatically spell irregular high-frequency words in their writing. The Words-We-Know Wall supports continuous correct use, since the words are available for reference. As a bi-product of building and using this Wall for writing, automaticity in reading these words is promoted.

All writers need to spell high-frequency words correctly; of course, you will want to take your class' developmental level into account. One way of dealing with develop-mental issues is to post fewer words on the Words-We-Know Wall at the kindergarten and first grade levels. Requiring first graders to correctly spell *the, of, a, to, you, was,* and *are,* all of which are in the top fifteen on frequency lists (Sitton, 1997; 1998), might be the extent of what most students at that level can successfully handle. An alternative is to build and use the Words-We-Know Wall with the 38 suggested words (see Chapter 2) in kindergarten and first grade without the expectation of mastery. By mid-second grade, the requirement can shift, making students accountable for correctly spelling all the words on the Wall.

In reading, the benefits of automaticity with high-frequency words are obvious. Because these words make up so much of what is read, stopping to process every *the, said,* and *have* greatly interferes with fluency and meaning making. Besides, these words cannot be sounded out. The sooner readers become automatic with such words, the better.

Although specific attention is often required to help writers spell these words correctly, reading and rereading appropriate materials is the main avenue for developing automatic recognition of high-frequency words. Thanks to the interconnected nature of reading and writing, those students who need extra help reading these words benefit from the spelling work we do with the Words-We-Know Wall.

Irregular High-Frequency Words

The following irregularly-spelled high-frequency words are listed in order of frequency according to the *American Heritage Word Frequency Book* (as cited in Adams, 1990, p. 274) and cross-referenced with *Rebecca Sitton's Spelling Sourcebook 1* (1996).

1. the	2. of	3. a	4. to	5. you
6. was	7. are	8. with	9. they	10. from
11. have	12. one	13. what	14. were	15. there
16. your	17. which	18. their	19. said	20. do
21. many	22. some	23. these	24. two	25. been
26. who	27. people	28. only	29. use	30. very
31. where	32. through	33. any	34. come	35. because
36. does	37. here	38. again		

(revised from Wagstaff, 1994, p. 25)

Building the Words-We-Know Wall

Expectations for building the Words-We-Know Wall differ at each grade level. In kindergarten, the goal may be to develop familiarity, targeting a few of the most frequent words for correctness. I wait a few months to begin the Wall, until students are attending to print, developing an understanding of the alphabetic principle, and recognizing the concept of word. We then add one or two words each week, after they have been noted repeatedly in reading. The plan may be similar in first grade, beginning the Wall after a few months and holding students accountable for some of the words. Another alternative is to focus on regularly spelled high-frequency words such as *and, in, that, it,* and *he* in kindergarten, and wait until first grade to concentrate on irregular words. Teachers working together may determine a plan for building accountability over time in grades K, 1, and 2. In second grade, we add two to three words each week in an effort to complete the Wall by mid-year; then, there is plenty of opportunity to practice these words correctly in writing. In terms of accountability, students may become responsible for spelling words correctly as they go up on the Words-We-Know Wall or once the Wall is complete. The second option allows more practice and time for writers to develop, but students should always be aware that they will be accountable for these words at some point.

Words for this Wall are written on colorful cards and trimmed according to word shape. Once harvested from a literacy context such as a poem, they may be directly added to the Words-We-Know Wall or practiced during the week with other Word Wall words before being posted. Words are organized in alphabetical order for easy reference.

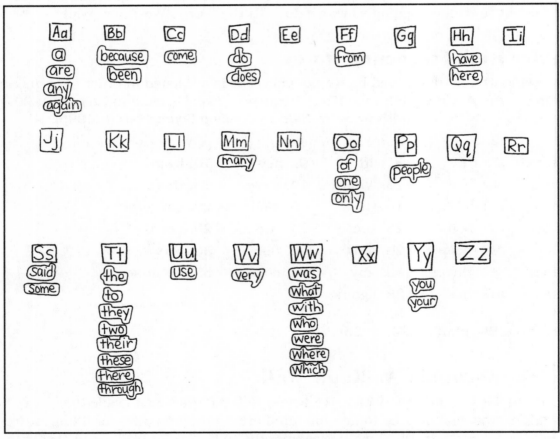

A K–1 wall

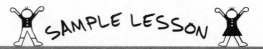

SAMPLE LESSON

Adding to the Words-We-Know Wall

The following example took place in a first grade classroom as a mini-lesson prior to writing workshop. A student's writing sample (see Figure 18) is used as the context for examining the word *the* and adding it to the Words-We-Know Wall. The word *the* is familiar since students have read and circled it repeatedly in the morning message, framed it during shared reading, and written it during interactive writing sessions.

Lesson Routine

A. Highlight the high frequency of the chosen word(s) in a student's writing sample, other writing context, or shared reading context.

B. Emphasize the correct spelling, counting the number of letters in the word and saying each letter as the word is written on a card.

C. Clarify correct spelling in the sample by going back to each instance, pointing to and naming each letter.

D. Allow students to search their own writing, highlighting each use of the word. Students can peer-edit, checking each instance of the word by pointing to and naming each letter with their partners.

E. Ask students to circle and edit their use of the word from now on in their writing. Continually praise students' correct use of the word in multiple writing contexts.

"Those are words we know how to spell."

Circling "things we know" in the morning message.

Makeing stew
In go the carrots,
In go the bunches of
streenbeans. In go the
buckets of tamatos.

figure 18

A. Highlight the high frequency of the chosen word(s) in a student's writing sample, other writing context, or shared reading context.

Teacher: I asked Rebecca if we could look at her writing today. Why don't you introduce us to your piece?

Rebecca: I got the idea for this story after we read *Stone Soup*. Sometimes I help my mom make stew, so I thought I could write about it.

Teacher: Would you like to read "Making Stew" to us?

(After Rebecca shared, students responded to her writing, first telling what they heard in her story, then asking questions and commenting.)

Teacher: Reading books often gives us ideas for stories. Something that happens may remind us of an event in our own lives or spark an idea. Rebecca decided to add some outrageous ingredients to her stew just like the cook did in *Stone Soup*.

(Following further comments, attention is shifted to the irregular high-frequency word *the*.)

B. Emphasize the correct spelling, counting the number of letters in the word and saying each letter as the word is written on a card.

(looking at Rebecca's writing on the overhead)

Teacher: Carla noticed how Rebecca's story followed a pattern. Did you notice how many times she wrote *the*? Let's count each *the* in her story. (Rebecca helps the class reread for *the*, underlining each instance.) *The* is one of those words writers use over and over. It isn't spelled like it sounds, so it is important to learn the right spelling. If Rebecca misspelled *the* over and over, she would be getting a lot of practice with the wrong spelling! We will add *the* to our Words-We-Know Wall so you can practice and learn the correct spelling. (I write *the* on a card, saying each letter.) Let's spell *the* together.

Students: T-h-e.

C. Clarify correct spelling in the sample by going back to each instance, pointing to and naming each letter.

Teacher: You noticed *the* has three letters, t-h-e. Every time you write *the*, make sure it has the same three letters, t-h-e. We underlined each *the* in Rebecca's story. Let's go back to each one and check the spelling, pointing to and saying each letter.

(Rebecca leads the class in checking each spelling.)

D. Allow students to search their own writing, highlighting each use of the word. Students can peer-edit, checking each instance of the word by pointing to and naming each letter with their partners.

Teacher: Now, let's see how often you use *the* in your writing. Take a piece of writing from your writing folder. Use your highlighter to mark each *the*. Then, check each spelling, pointing to and saying each letter just like we did with Rebecca's writing. Work with a partner to find and check each *the* in your writing.

(As students work I circulate, commenting on how often they are finding *the* and how they are doing with checking the spelling. After a few minutes, the class comes together to discuss their findings.)

Teacher: What did you notice about *the*?

Students: We found it twelve times!

Students: We found it more than that.

Students: I kept forgetting the *e* at the end.

Students: I think I will spell it right now.

Teacher: You can see how often you write *the*. Since it is so important to learn the right spelling, we'll add it to the Words-We-Know Wall for you to check. Good writers try to spell these words correctly because they know it makes their pieces easier to read. Imagine trying to read someone's writing who misspelled these words over and over! Besides, you don't want to get a lot of practice with the wrong spelling. When you turn in a piece for me to edit, you can circle and check *the* along with other things you know you've done well in your writing.

E. Ask students to circle and edit their use of the word from now on in their writing. Continually praise students' correct use of the word in multiple writing contexts.

Following the lesson, the class begins independent writing. During the next several days, and recurrently thereafter, I call attention to students who circle and correctly spell *the*, along with other Words We Know.

Things to Remember

- I frequently use the morning message, interactive and shared writing, and student samples for harvesting words for the Words-We-Know Wall. We take examples *from* writing for students to apply *in* writing.

- One of the best ways to reinforce use of the Words-We-Know Wall is to continually praise students for finding, highlighting, editing, and correctly spelling words from the Words-We-Know Wall. Having students search and circle encourages responsibility for evaluating their work. Those who are ready may develop personal goals for mastering words on the Words-We-Know Wall, evaluating their own progress by checking off each time a word is used consistently correctly on their own word list. Periodically, they may also take a partner spelling test.

- When adding a reference to the Words-We-Know Wall, you might demonstrate each word's utility by having students hunt for it for a week. They search their own writing and any reading materials. Each time the word is found, a tally is made on a tally sheet. At the end of the week, tally up and emphasize the importance of the word!

- Responsibility should increase with older and more able students. Although first graders may be asked to spell these words correctly, receiving praise and recognition for doing so, by mid-second grade and beyond students should be required to spell the words correctly all the time. Any writing sample from any area of the curriculum may be checked. Students missing words from the Words-We-Know Wall should not be eligible for a top spelling grade (Sitton, 1996; 1998).

Meeting Individual Needs

The biggest adaptations here are the number of words added to the Words-We-Know Wall at one time, procedures for checking the words, and the degree of student responsibility. As you add words to the Words-We-Know Wall, watch students' writings. If they are consistently spelling the words correctly, you may try adding several words at once. Conversely, if students are struggling to meet the standard, you probably have too many words and need to slow down. Start off slowly. It is always easier to add words than to decrease the number.

The procedure for editing for Words We Know may vary. Younger, less experienced writers need a lot of structure, such as in the lesson example. By second grade, it may be sufficient to have students simply circle or underline Words We Know, visually checking the whole word rather than each letter. Older primary grade students can check a box on an editing checklist to indicate they have edited for Words We Know. Regardless of the approach, it must be modeled and practiced for student success. Make a point of occasionally editing your own writing sample, modeling the expected behavior.

MID-WEEK PRACTICE ACTIVITIES

Students use highlighting tape to call attention to Words We Know in interactive writing.

- **Frame Words:** Students frame, circle, and highlight Words We Know in shared and guided reading and writing.

- **Read Patterned Books:** Students read and reread high-frequency words in patterned, predictable materials such as Scholastic's *My Books* for kindergarten and first grade.

- **Read the Room:** Students match high-frequency words written on self-sticking notes to words around the room.

- **Pocket Charts:** Students put these words together when reassembling text in pocket charts. After writing text for the pocket chart on sentence strips, cut irregular high-frequency words apart from the rest of the sentence (so you have the word on a card). Initially, cut out whole words to reinforce reading when they are placed back in the context of the sentence. Later, cut these words into letter pieces to reinforce spelling.

A pocket chart

- **Morning Message:** Students circle the week's Words-We-Know words in the morning message.

- **Text Innovations:** When innovating patterned texts, students practice writing irregular high-frequency words (i.e., Brown bear, brown bear, **what do you see?** Black cat, black cat, **what do you see?**).

- **Magnetic Board:** Students make one or two words using magnetic letters or letter cards. They scramble the letters and remake the words, working on increasing speed and accuracy. As each word is made, have students say the letters, then run their fingers under the completed word, reading it aloud.

- **Edit:** Students work with partners to edit their writing drafts, looking for specific words from the Words-We-Know Wall. Each example is highlighted and checked. Students touch and say each letter, cross-checking the Wall. You may determine one, two, or three words to focus on during each session. For example, "Today, use your highlighter to find each *you* and *the* in your writing. Work with your partner to touch and say each letter, checking each spelling." Older or more experienced students circle and edit all words from the Words-We-Know Wall in their drafts.

"I know how to spell it (the). It's on the Wall."

- **Quick Review:** Do a quick review a few times each week. Take five to ten minutes to call out words from the Words-We-Know Wall for students to spell on scratch paper. After each word is called out, clap the letters, then have students point to each letter to check the spelling, circling errors. Respell the word together as students rewrite it. As students gain experience, let them take turns leading the review.

- **Rainbow Writing:** Try rainbow writing. Students write the word in one color and check the spelling. Then, they write over the word in another color and say each letter, working on speed and accuracy. Repeat with more colors.

- **Point it Out:** Students use big pointers to read and spell words on the Words-We-Know Wall during learning center or reading workshop time.

- **Fill in the Blanks:** Students fill in blank spaces in the Morning Message with words from the Words-We-Know Wall, thereby reviewing spelling and meaning in context (i.e., Dear boys and girls, We will h____ (have) a picnic today. Did ____ (you) bring a sack lunch?).

- **Sing the Wall:** My students liked the rhythm and words of *I Like the Rain* so much that they wanted to try spelling new words to the song. Someone suggested we "sing the Words-We-Know Wall," so we adapted the lyrics. Students take turns using a yardstick to point to a word on the Wall and sing along with the book on tape.

We know <u>the</u>.
We know <u>the</u>.
How do you spell it?
T-h-e, (clap)
We know <u>the</u>.

We know <u>they</u>.
We know <u>they</u>.
How do you spell it?
T-h-e-y
We know they.

END OF WEEK

The Words-We-Know Wall words can be added as you harvest them, or you can wait until the end of the week to affix them to the Wall.

Connecting the Words-We-Know Wall to Reading and Writing

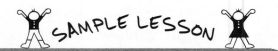

Using the Words-We-Know Wall During Writing

In this lesson, I quickly review the standard form of a letter while modeling use of the Words-We-Know Wall.

Lesson Routine

A. Negotiate text with students or think aloud while writing your own text.

B. Refer to the Words-We-Know Wall to

check spelling of irregular high-frequency words.

C. Reread often.

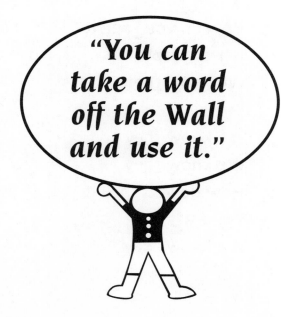

"You can take a word off the Wall and use it."

A. Negotiate text with students or think aloud while writing your own text.

Teacher: We are enjoying the new books Ms. Johns donated to our library. Now we have more than one copy of some of our favorites and many new titles! I thought it would be a good idea to write her a thank-you letter. What do you think?

(after hearing students' responses)

Teacher: What should we say in the letter? Remember our purpose for writing is to thank her for the books. Tell your neighbor what you think we should include.

(Students share with a peer, suggestions are discussed, and the letter is begun on chart paper.)

Teacher: Letters usually begin with the date and a greeting. We can write the date here (pointing upper left, writing the date). What greeting should we use?

Student: Dear Ms. Johns.

Teacher: Okay, the greeting goes under the date. I need a capital to start and capitals for the name. Dear Ms. Johns. I also need a comma after the greeting. Now what?

Student: Thank you for the books.

B. Refer to the Words-We-Know Wall to check spelling of irregular high-frequency words.

Teacher: I'm going to indent, moving my pen in a few spaces to begin the body of the letter. (I write.) I need a capital to start the sentence. Thank you (pause). Now *you* is one of the Words We Know. Let me check the Words-We-Know Wall to make sure I get the correct spelling. I need to look under *y* on the Wall. Yes, it is y-o-u. Good spellers check the Wall to make sure these words are spelled correctly. Wait! *The* is another Word We Know. I write it so often, I think I know the right spelling—t-h-e. Let me check the Words-We-Know Wall to be sure. Yes, under *t, the* is t-h-e. Okay, thank you for the books. What should we add?

Students: We read them.

Students: How about, we are busy reading them?

Teacher: Yes, I think Ms. Johns would like to hear we are putting the books to good use. So, (beginning to write) I need another capital to start the sentence, *We are.* Oh! *Are* is another Word We Know. Let me check the Words-We-Know Wall, this one can be tricky! *Are,* a-r-e (pointing to the word on the Wall), okay (writing) a-r-e, we are busy reading them. I need a period to end the sentence.

C. Reread often.

Teacher: Good writers reread to make sure their writing says what they want it to say and to make changes. Let's reread (pointing).

Dear Ms. Johns, Thank you for the books. We are busy reading them. Any changes? What else can we say?"

Students: Let's tell her about the books we like.

Students: I like the *Curious George* books.

Students: I like the book *Lunch*!

Teacher: I'm sure we all have many favorites!

Students: We can't say all the books we like!

Students: We could say we have lots of favorites!

Teacher: Okay, let's see, (beginning to write) *We*, I started the sentence with a capital, *have* (pause). *Have* is another word we use a lot that isn't spelled like it sounds. Let me check the Words-We-Know Wall. *Have*, /h/, it must be under *h*. Yes, *have*, h-a-v-e, (continuing to write) lots of favorites. I'll put an exclamation point at the end of the sentence to show our excitement.

Student: *Of* is on the Wall, too.

Teacher: Can you check the spelling for us?

Student: We have lots of, o-f.

Teacher: Great! Anything else to tell Ms. Johns?

Students: Why don't we ask her to come read to us?

Teacher: I bet she'd like that! Okay, (rereading) Dear Ms. Johns, thank you for the books. We are busy reading them. We have lots of favorites! Would you come read to us? Does that sound good?

Students: Yeah!

Teacher: How should we close the letter?

Students: From our class.

Students: Love, Room 25.

Students: We have to say which class!

Teacher: Right, we want to be specific so she knows whom the letter is from. Let's go with 'Love, Room 25.' Okay, I need to put the closing down here (pointing and beginning to write). I need a capital for the closing. Capital *L*, love... I need a comma, Room 25. Let's reread, making sure our letter says what we want and that the Words We Know look right. Then, you can sign the letter.

Things to Remember

- It's so simple to model using the Words-We-Know Wall. Imagine the power of continually referencing the Wall to review the spellings of these words. It becomes a habit for you and your students. The words become overlearned and automaticity is achieved.

- Students learn and review so much when teachers think aloud as they write! In this example, using the Words-We-Know Wall was emphasized. The teacher may have thought aloud about any number of things. Certainly every irregular, high-frequency word does not have to be referenced in a piece of writing.

- Note how quickly references to capitals and end marks are made. "I need a capital to start my sentence, I need a capital for a name, I need a question mark here because I'm asking a question." Just a few words as the writing proceeds reviews these important concepts over and over in the real context of writing. (For more information, see Chapter 4, The Help Wall.)

Meeting Individual Needs

Thinking aloud is such a flexible technique. In this lesson, we negotiated the text together. Try thinking aloud while composing your own pieces. Model writing for different purposes and with different genres. Try a memo to another teacher, note to a friend, learning log entry, book or movie review, letter to the principal, report on a topic students are studying, entry for the class newsletter, invitation for a class event, or innovation on a favorite story or poem.

Consider the length of the text and your students' abilities. If the text is lengthy, try shorter, frequent spurts of writing. Continue thinking aloud and making additions over the course of a few days. This way, students' attention is maintained, and they benefit from seeing how a writer stops and returns to a piece.

"**Because is spelled funny!**"

More Ways to Use the Words-We-Know Wall

Modeled Writing: Use any topic and any writing genre to model using the Words-We-Know Wall during writing. Remember, variety is the key!

Recording the Daily News: One of my students noted, "We use these words every day in the news!" This activity reinforces the importance of the Words-We-Know Wall.

Journal Writing: Compose a journal entry in front of students referring to the Words-We-Know Wall.

Writing Workshop: Students circle and check Words We Know during writing workshop. Spell checking is frequently modeled in student samples and in teacher-authored pieces. Correct spelling of Words We Know is recognized and celebrated.

Content-Area Writing: Keep the standard during all writing activities throughout the day. Model and reinforce correct spelling.

REMEMBER: Anytime you write is an appropriate time to refer to and model use of the Words-We-Know Wall.

CLASSROOM SNAPSHOTS

Grade Appropriate Words-We-Know Walls

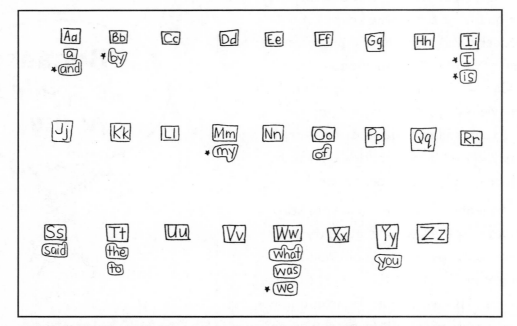

Kindergarten Words-We-Know Wall: This example includes some regularly spelled high-frequency words (starred).

Teaching Reading & Writing with Word Walls • Scholastic Professional Books

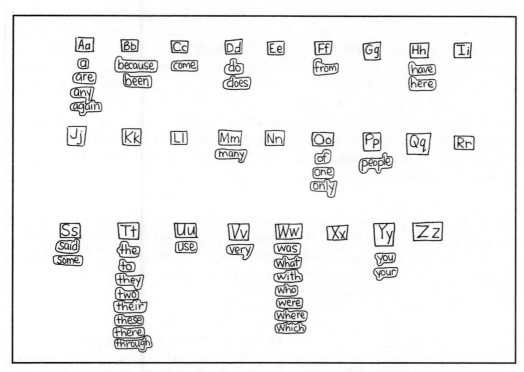

Second Grade Words-We-Know Wall: This same wall is used in third grade on up.

FINAL THOUGHTS

Getting students to spell high-frequency words correctly in their daily writing is not as difficult as it may sound. Rather than including these words on the Friday spelling test, expecting transfer, model and reinforce the correct spelling in the context of real writing. Work continually with the Words-We-Know Wall. Make using the Wall a part of what you do every day.

Provide parents with a list of the Words We Know and explain your expectations. Encourage them to share the responsibility for helping their children learn these words. Interest intermediate grade teachers in maintaining the Words We Know standard. Provide them with a list of these words. Older students may keep copies in their desks or writing folders, checking the list as necessary or, as required, editing for their drafts.

Assessing correct use of the Words We Know does not need to be overwhelming. No one can check every piece of writing every child does every day! Spot checking is sufficient for communicating your intent. You might check a few papers each day, getting to all students in a week's time. Keep dated notations in your grade book, such as a + for a correct sample and a – for a sample with misspellings. Take particular note of students whose writing continually contains misspellings of Words-We-Know Wall words. List the words they are missing in their writing folders, alert parents, and involve them in the specific review activities noted in the Mid-week Practice Activities section.

An alternative for tracking use of the Words We Know is to make a high-frequency word spreadsheet (Hayward, 1998). List the words on the Words-We-Know Wall under each child's name. As samples are reviewed, highlight the words used consistently correctly. Those that remain unhighlighted over time become the focus of specific mini-lessons and review.

Use your professional judgment when creating and adding to the Words-We-Know Wall. If your students are early emergent spellers, representing words with one or two letters, they are probably not ready for the Words-We-Know Wall. Likewise, if students are continually missing posted words, slow down and work with what you have. Keep a developmental perspective and work with your colleagues to meet the goal of standard spelling for all 38 irregular high-frequency words by mid-second grade. You can do it and so can your students!

"We check our writing to make sure those words are right."

CHAPTER FOUR

The Help Wall

I use capitals for names and places

remember apostrophes, commas, and spaces

know the difference between to, two, and too

and use them in everyday writing, do you?

I use question marks, periods, and exclamations

drop the *e*, add *es*, and remember quotations

I know them, I use them, one and all

It's easy! I write and reference the Wall!

—J.W.

The Help Wall is a reference for language conventions such as punctuation marks, capitalization, homonyms, contractions, words that undergo spelling changes when suffixes are added, and any other tricky points for developing writers. Key words, phrases, and sentences, accompanied by picture clues, are organized on the Wall in categories (i.e., all punctuation examples grouped together, all references for capitals grouped together) or in any manner that makes sense to students.

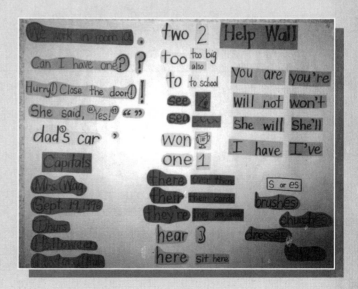

As students demonstrate the need for a skill, it is modeled and discussed in multiple contexts. Once familiar with the skill, a reference is posted on the Help Wall. References for capitalization and punctuation are usually the first on the Wall. Use of the Help Wall is demonstrated throughout the day during modeled and interactive writing. These language conventions and other skills are then practiced in context during daily writing workshop and content area writing.

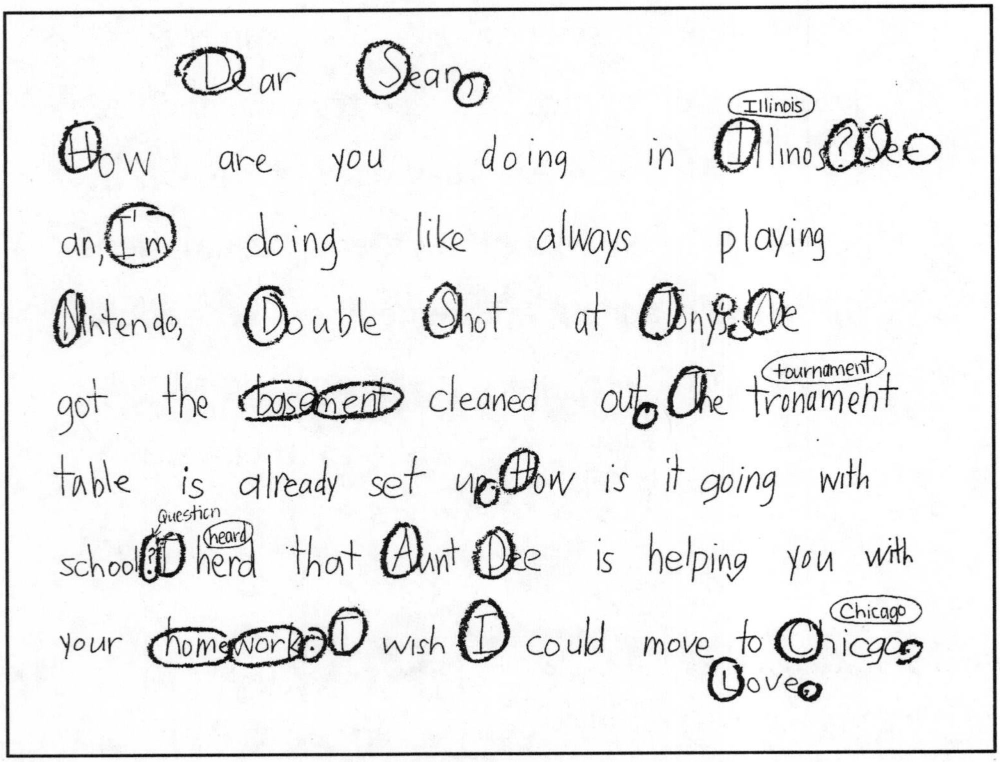

figure 21

Once a reference is posted, students are encouraged to look for use of the skill in their own writing and circle it. We call this "circling the things we know in our writing." (See Figure 21.) By circling, students become responsible for using the skill and for celebrating their successes. This is a positive approach to editing. Instead of saying, "Go back and look for the things you've done wrong and fix them," I say, "Circle the things you know you've done well in your writing. Use the Help Wall as a reminder of the things you know." In the process of noting their skill use, students notice mistakes. They often fix them and circle them as something they've done well. Students learn to apply conventions through correct continuous use of skills in their writing. The Help Wall is a way of supporting this continuous use.

GETTING STARTED

Purposes of the Help Wall

I've used Help Walls with students to:

- increase students' use of conventions and basic skills in process writing

- provide a user-friendly reference for developing use of language conventions

We want all students to apply developmentally appropriate skills and conventions in their writing. Usually this goal begins in first grade with a focus on using capitals and end marks. Again, the needs and abilities of students must be considered. The work they do in writing leads the way in determining what goes on the Help Wall.

When I began teaching, I taught writing conventions and skills with worksheets. Although students seemed to be learning—they scored well on practice exercises and were able to pass unit tests—few correctly used capitals, end mark punctuation, contractions, and other language conventions in their everyday writing. Realizing my teaching approach had to change, I began using techniques for teaching and modeling skills and conventions during actual writing events. These included thinking aloud when I wrote, circling conventions in the morning message, composing the daily news, and conferencing with students.

The successes we experienced building and using Word Walls as references led me to consider creating the Help Wall. Now, as we compose the daily news or write interactively, we have meaningful examples to help us use language conventions and remind us of tricky spelling changes. The Help Wall documents our explicit work with conventions and skills from writing workshop mini-lessons. We continually refer to it and use it as we write. Through constant use in meaningful contexts, students come to truly understand and apply these skills in their writing.

Building the Wall

In grades 1 and 2, I recommend beginning a Help Wall a few months into the school year. This allows time for students to "buy into" writing workshop and feel success without undue worry about specific conventions and skills. Naturally, we work with skills and conventions during these first months as we record the daily news, read the morning message, and write throughout the day, but my main concern as the year begins has generally been on other writing issues. These include procedural issues for starting the writing workshop, methods for topic generation, and identifying qualities of good writing. In third grade and beyond, teachers begin the Help Wall sooner, since students generally are more advanced writers.

References are added to the Help Wall after a skill or convention has been modeled and discussed in multiple contexts. For example, after observing the need for students to use end mark punctuation, we circle periods, question marks, and exclamations in the morning message; frame or highlight end marks during shared reading; and note end marks during interactive writing and the daily news. In each case, we quickly discuss the proper end mark and why it was used. Once familiar, we decide on appropriate references to add to the Help Wall. Although we may collect multiple examples of sentences ending with periods, question marks, and exclamation points on a chart, just one reference for each is posted. This keeps the Help Wall less cluttered and more user-friendly.

The number of references depends on what can be expected developmentally to appear in students' writing. A Help Wall in first grade is less complex than one in second grade, third grade, and so on.

Unlike with the ABC and Chunking Walls, I do not use a weekly time frame for adding to the Help Wall. As a particular skill or convention becomes familiar, we add it to the Wall. Students are then encouraged to look for and circle its use in their own writing.

SAMPLE LESSON

Adding to the Help Wall

The following lesson precedes writing workshop. An overhead of one of my writing samples is used to highlight the convention of capitalizing names.

Lesson Routine

A. Note (frame, circle, highlight, discuss) a particular skill or convention in varied reading and writing contexts to build familiarity. Discuss the need for the skill or convention.

B. Cooperatively decide on a reference. Determine an appropriate place to post the reference (category or other).

C. Ask students to begin circling their use of this skill or convention in their writing. Regularly recognize students' efforts in using and identifying the skill or convention.

A. Note (frame, circle, highlight, discuss) a particular skill or convention in varied reading and writing contexts to build familiarity. Discuss the need for the skill or convention.

Teacher: We've noticed how writers capitalize names in the books we've been reading and have worked on using capitals for names in the daily news. Some of you are remembering to capitalize names in your stories and letters in writing workshop and throughout the day in other writing. Today, let's add something to our Help Wall to help us remember to capitalize names whenever we write. What shall we post to help us?

B. Cooperatively decide on a reference. Determine an appropriate place to post the reference (category or other).

(The students and I agree on a common reference. This may be a name of a student or favorite storybook character. In the past, my students suggested posting Mrs. Wag with circles around the capitals, since they were accustomed to seeing my name and circling the capitals in the morning message.)

Teacher: Where should we post *Mrs. Wag* on the Help Wall?

(My students and I often categorize references. *Mrs. Wag* would be posted with other references for capitalization.)

C. Ask students to begin circling their use of this skill or convention in their writing. Regularly recognize students' efforts in using and identifying the skill or convention.

Teacher: Now that the reference for capitalizing names is on the Help Wall, try to capitalize names in your own writing and circle your use of capitals when you go back to "circle the things you know when you write." Let's look at a piece of my writing.

(My writing sample is put on the overhead. I think aloud searching for names, checking for capitalization, and circling each example. Other examples of "things we know" are also circled, referencing the Help Wall.)

Things to Remember

- Involve students in deciding what reference to post for any particular skill or convention. If the reference is meaningful to them, they are more likely to remember it and use the Help Wall. Examples often come from our shared literature experiences. We use this context to build familiarity before a reference is posted.

- I frequently use my own writing to model searching and circling "things we know." I choose drafts that repeatedly exemplify the concept we're adding to the Help Wall. In this case, an article for our class newsletter was used, since it contained many names.

- Using the overhead, have volunteers model searching their own samples, referencing the Help Wall, and circling things they know. Remember to recognize and celebrate students who are using skills and conventions in their everyday writing. Show their samples as positive examples on the overhead.

Meeting Individual Needs

One variable to consider when adapting this lesson is the amount of time needed to build familiarity with a concept before it is added to the Help Wall. In the primary grades, more time is needed than in intermediate grades, since younger students have had less experience with language conventions.

As with other Word Walls, the number of references and the speed at which they're added depend on your students. Don't overwhelm them by requiring too much too early. Begin slowly. Add to the Help Wall as students demonstrate continual use of the references already posted. Additionally, get those intermediate grade teachers involved! Show them your Help Wall, discuss expectations, and encourage them to continue the practice, making appropriate additions. Many intermediate students still need the support of the Help Wall to meet the goal of correct continuous use of language conventions in their writing.

MID-WEEK PRACTICE ACTIVITIES

- **Frame Words:** Continually note how writers use skills during shared reading. Circle, frame, highlight, or underline conventions to quickly draw attention to a specific aspect of the text. Circle, frame, and highlight conventions in multiple contexts including the morning message, Big Books, text on the overhead, shared reading posters, the daily news, and shared or interactive writing charts.

- **Collect Words:** Students search reading and writing contexts to collect examples of language conventions and record them on charts. You might create individual charts for capitalized names, capitalized places, sentences ending with question marks, sentences ending with exclamation points, favorite quotes, sentences using homophones, words ending in -es, and other skills. You can use the charts to build familiarity with the conventions and eventually select the best example for the Help Wall.

- **Model Writing:** Continually reference the Help Wall during shared and modeled writing. Think aloud as you and the students write.

- **Circle in Drafts.** Require students to circle their use of skills and conventions in their writing drafts.

- **Overhead Celebrations:** Celebrate successes. Show positive examples of convention usage by copying and displaying student writing samples on the overhead.

Connecting the Help Wall to Writing

SAMPLE LESSON

Using the Help Wall During Writing (Lesson Routine)

A. Students share their news orally in small groups. Choose a few to share with the whole class.

B. Record one student's news. Students call out as teacher writes.

C. Refer to the Help Wall to cross check correct use of writing skills and conventions.

D. Make the news available for rereading.

A. Students share their news orally in small groups. Choose a few to share with the whole class.

When it is daily news time, we often form "buzz groups" of three or four children, so everyone has a chance to share news from their lives. During sharing, I circulate, "listening for stories" or possible topic ideas for writing workshop. After a few minutes, we come together as a group. Two or three students share their news with the class. Usually the news shared by the first student is recorded on chart paper. As we record the news, we frequently refer to the Help Wall.

Teacher: I heard a lot of interesting news in buzz groups today. Who would like to share with the class?

Student: I'm moving to my aunt's house in Millcreek.

Teacher: Oh! Cathy's family is moving! That's right, I heard you put your house up for sale. But you will finish the year with us here, right?

Student: Yes. After school is out, we will move to Millcreek while the new house is being built.

Teacher: Moving and building a new house can be very exciting. Remember Craig brought in pictures of his new house as it was being built? Cathy could do the same thing and write about her experience. Moving involves many experiences that may make good writing topics. Can you think of any?

Students: Getting a new room.

Students: How it is to make new friends.

Students: Going to a new school.

Teacher: All of those experiences could be included in a story about moving, or they could each be a topic of their own. Cathy will have to give that some thought. Who else would like to share some news?

Student: My team won its first baseball game!

(The class discusses the student's news, asking questions and linking experiences to possible writing topics.)

B. Record one student's news. Students call out as teacher writes.

Teacher: Okay, let's record Cathy's news. Help us remember Cathy, you said, "I'm moving to my aunt's house in Millcreek," right? How shall we start?

(Students call out responses as I write on chart paper.)

Student: We could start with Cathy said . . .

Teacher: Yes. Since we use *said* so often, let's think of synonyms. Cathy...

Students: Yelled.

Students: Cried.

Students: Whined.

Students: Exclaimed.

Teacher: All of those convey a different feeling. Which one fits, Cathy?

Cathy: Cried.

Teacher: So, we'll begin with 'Cathy cried.' Help me out...

Students: Capital C—a-t-h-y.

Teacher: Yes, we need a capital here, because we're starting a sentence and writing a name. Help me out with *cried*.

Students: C-r-y-e-d.

Students: C-r-i-e-d.

C. Refer to the Help Wall to cross check correct use of writing skills and conventions.

Teacher: I hear two different spellings. Let's check the Help Wall. Do you see any other words like *cry* that might help us decide how to correctly add the ending *-ed*?

Students: Try.

Teacher: What do you notice?

Students: For *tries,* we changed the *y* to *i* before we added the ending.

Teacher: *Try* is like *cry*. There is a consonant before the *y*. We also have *fly* and *carry* on the Help Wall. We changed the *y* to *i* before each ending was added. So, how should we spell *cried*?

Students: C-r-i-e-d.

Teacher: Okay, "Cathy cried". . Help me out.

Students: Comma, quotation.

Teacher: Yes. We need a comma here after the name and a quotation mark here as we begin to record what is being said just like on our Help Wall with *Pierre said*—comma, quotation. What next?

Students: Capital *I* apostrophe *m*.

Teacher: We need a capital to start the sentence that Cathy is saying. Besides, we know *I* is always capitalized when it is written by itself. Why do we need an apostrophe? Tell your neighbor.

(I listen as students share.)

Teacher: I heard you say it's right on the Help Wall. Yes, *I'm* is a contraction. We are writing *I am*. We need an apostrophe to take the place of the letter *a*. So, we have Cathy cried, "I'm moving . . . " (pause for student response)

Students: M-o-v-i-n-g.

Teacher: Yes, *moving* is like *skating, traded,* and *sliding*. We drop the *e* before we add an ending.

Students: T-o, m-y.

Teacher: Yes, (rereading) "I'm moving to my aunt's house". . . Help me.

Students: A-n-t-s.

Students: A-u-n-t-s.

Students: A-u-n-t- apostrophe s.

Teacher: I'm hearing different responses. First, which spelling is correct, a-n-t or a-u-n-t? It's a homonym. Let's look at our references on the Help Wall. It's not there. Can anyone think of something they know that may help us?

Student: We read *The Ant and the Elephant* (pointing to the book). The little insect is a-n-t like in the book.

Student: We'll, it's not that ant! We're talking about Cathy's aunt!

Teacher: Yes, good thinking! Using the book you know was a great way to figure out the right spelling, (writing) a-u-n-t. Who would like to add *ant* and *aunt* to our homonym chart?

Student: I can draw an ant next to a-n-t.

Student: Write 'Cathy's aunt' next to a-u-n-t.

Teacher: OK, is it a-u-n-t-s or a-u-n-t apostrophe *s*? Use the Help Wall and tell your neighbor what you think. (after talk time) Who will share?

Student: It's apostrophe *s* because it's her aunt's house.

Teacher: Yes, if we just add *s*, it means more than one aunt—many aunts. Apostrophe *s* is like *dad's car* on our Help Wall, it shows ownership. (writing) So, we need apostrophe *s* to show it is

Cathy's aunt's house. Okay, *house* like *mouse*.

Students: H-o-u-s-e.

Teacher: in Millcreek.

Students: i-n capital *M*.

Teacher: Capital *M* because it's the name of a place like Salt Lake City. *Mill* like *pill*.

Students: i-l-l-c-r-e-e-k period.

Teacher: Yes, we need a period to end the sentence, then what do I need here? (pointing to the chart)

Students: Quotation mark.

Students: Like at the end of *Pierre said, "I don't care."*

D. Make the news available for rereading.

Teacher: Right! We need a quotation to mark the end of what Cathy said. Our reference on the Wall is *Pierre said,* comma, quotation, *"I don't care."* Period, quotation. You're all doing such a good job of remembering capitals, commas, and quotations in your writing! Okay, let's reread, making sure everything looks and sounds right.

Things to Remember

- This lesson was videotaped in May in my second grade classroom. Recording the daily news took approximately five minutes. By this time, students were quite skilled at using the conventions and skills on the Help Wall since they had been practicing all year.

- Notice how natural it is to reference more than one Wall while writing. Here, the Help Wall was handy for many basic skills and conventions. We made analogies to words on the Chunking Wall as we spelled *Millcreek* and *house*. Also, we often used the Words-We-Know Wall to spell high-frequency words. Although I have discussed the Walls separately for each chapter of this book, we commonly reference all of them as we complete a piece of writing.

- As you write the daily news or other text, you certainly do not have to reference every convention or skill in the piece. Continuous quick review supports students' use of conventions and skills in everyday writing. Keep in mind the many writing contexts throughout the day available for modeling and using the Help Wall.

- While writing, if you come across the need for a convention or skill not referenced on the Help Wall, provide one to fit the immediate need. Then initiate a hunt. As examples are collected, familiarity is gained. Continue to note the convention or skill as you read and write in multiple contexts. Then, agree on a common reference to post on the Help Wall.

Meeting Individual Needs

Students of all ages enjoy sharing and recording their news. The daily news is a favorite for rereading since it relates directly to the students. The method for recording the daily news may be adapted to provide varying degrees of student support. When teachers think aloud and write, students have the least responsibility and the most support. As students call out or share the pen, the responsibility is shared. Older or more advanced students may take full responsibility, assuming the role of the teacher and recording the daily news as others call out. Cooperative groups may also try recording the daily news, comparing their versions to check for proper use of conventions and skills. It is fun to check these versions on the overhead, recording a final corrected version for rereading on chart paper.

More Ways to Use the Help Wall

Modeled Writing: You can use any topic and any genre to model use of the Help Wall. Remember, variety is critical.

Highlight: Use highlighting tape, frames or sticky notes to emphasize correct use of capitals, periods, quotes, and so forth, in Big Books, on charts, or any other shared reading context. "Look how these authors used...correctly in their writing."

Journal Writing: Compose a journal entry in front of students. Refer to the Help Wall to model use of correct grammar, usage, and mechanics skills.

Interactive Writing: It's natural to reference the Help Wall when dealing with proper use of skills and conventions during interactive writing. As you "share the pen" with students, have them check capitalization, add punctuation marks, cross-check to correctly spell homonyms, and note other aspects of the text.

Writing Workshop: Students circle "things they know" during Writing Workshop. Correct use of skills and conventions is recognized and celebrated.

REMEMBER: Anytime you write is an appropriate time to refer to and model use of the Help Wall.

CLASSROOM SNAPSHOTS

Grade Appropriate Help Walls

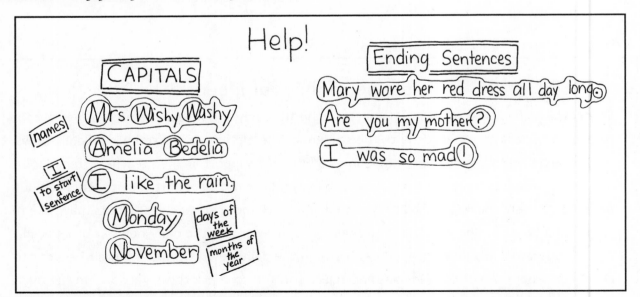

figure 22: First grade Help Wall in progress.

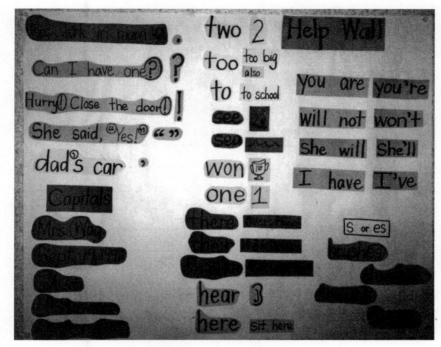

figure 23: Second grade Help Wall in progress.

FINAL THOUGHTS

If you want to improve your students' abilities to use skills and conventions in everyday writing, try building and using a Help Wall. Lessons like those described in this chapter have made a great difference in the overall look of literacy in my students' writing. They understand *why, when,* and *how* to use skills and conventions because constant modeling in authentic writing contexts coupled with the support of relevant references enables real application. Before, we practiced with rote exercises. Now, our practice occurs in daily writing!

During individual or small-group writing conferences, I review what students have done well as writers, including their use of skills and conventions. One column of my writing conference record is devoted to noting "things we know." After responding to the content of the piece, I always ask students to share the "things they know they've done well," tying into the skills and conventions they have circled. These are listed on the record. As the list grows, we look back and survey growth. The writing conference record and dated writing samples are shared with parents to communicate progress. Figure 24 shows a conference record based on David's writing sample (see next page).

Writing Conference Record

name date title	things I do as a writer	skills/strategies used	skills/strategies encouraged

David
2/12/97
letter to
Sean
	Using varied genre-
	letter format
	
	Considering audience-
	writing appropriate
	content to cousin
		Caps to start sentences
		Caps for proper nouns-
		   Sean, Nintendo,
		Double Shot, Tony's, Aunt
		Dee, Chicago, Illinois
		Apostrophe use-- I'm,
		   Tony's
		Periods to end sentences
		Many conventional spellings
		and use of Words We
		know --
		   to, are, with, you, the
			Proper use of question
			marks
			Help Wall for homonyms--
			   herd + heard
			   (added to personal
			   sp. dictionary)

figure 24

Another means of tracking progress is to keep a spreadsheet of skills and conventions on the Help Wall. Under each child's name, list specific skills such as *capitalizes the beginning of sentences, capitalizes names, uses periods,* and *uses question marks.* As you review writing samples, highlight the skill or convention used consistently correctly under each student's name. Those that remain unhighlighted over time can be the focus of mini-lessons and individualized goals (adapted from Hayward, 1998).

CHAPTER FIVE

Other Word Walls

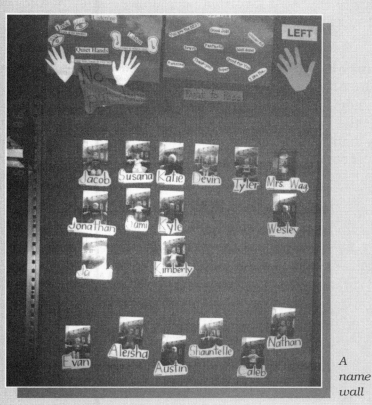

A name wall

> Interpret and innovate. Create Word Walls that reflect your unique teaching style.

Word Walls may serve many purposes in your classroom. The following are a few additional ideas that may meet your students' needs and stimulate your own Word Wall adaptations.

The Title Wall

Titles are memorable. They are easily recalled just like repetitive phrases in favorite books—even very young children request titles by name. Titles are accessible to almost everyone. Why not use the words in titles as the basis for learning about words and sounds?

Building and using a Title Wall is a simple, natural extension of the "read to" and "read with" experiences common in classrooms today. Teachers universally recognize—and research supports—the value of reading aloud to children. Daily shared reading is a part of language arts programs in most primary grades. Frequently, read alouds and shared readings are repeated. Students often revisit these books independently. The titles of repeated favorites become well-known, and words that are well-known make the best references.

Titles of favorite books may be written on sentence strips or colored butcher paper and listed on the wall alphabetically. A copy of an illustration from each book may accompany the titles. Underline either beginning letters or rimes depending on your purpose. For example, after reading Dr. Seuss' *Hop on Pop* in kindergarten, I record the title with the letters *h* and *p* underlined to highlight them. The same title might be recorded in a first or second grade classroom with the *-op* chunk underlined.

figure 25

Model making analogies to beginning sounds in the words underlined in the titles, just as you would use words on the ABC Wall. (See Figure 25.) For example, "I'm describing the funny crook in my cat's tail. Let's see, tail, *t-t-tail*. I hear /t/ like *t-t-t-teddy* from *Teddy Bear, Teddy Bear*. *Tail* must start with the letter *t*. I also hear /l/ like *Lllunch*. I must need *l* at the end. I'll leave a dash in the middle of the word for the other letters." Or, model making analogies to the chunks in words underlined in the titles, just as you would use key words on the Chunking Wall. (See Figure 26.) For example, "I know *-ark* like in *dark* (pointing to the word *dark* in the title *In A Dark, Dark Wood*) and *-ing* like in *things* (pointing to the word *things* in the title *Where the Wild Things Are*). This word must be *parking*!" Techniques for modeling the use of the Title Wall are the same as those described in Chapters 1 and 2.

figure 26

The Name Wall

Names can help students learn the ABCs and use analogies to read and write new words. Add student names to the Wall a few at a time, reinforcing the beginning sound as you would other ABC Wall words. Write the names on sentence strips or cards. Review spellings and sounds by cutting the names into letters. Allow volunteers to "be the letters," reassembling the names in front of the class. Make analogies to the names on the Wall during reading and writing. For example, while sharing the pen to write the daily news, you might say, "Today. . . t-t-t-today. I hear /t/ like *Tina*. Tina, would you like to come up and record a *t* to begin the word *today*? (as Tina writes) What else do you hear in *today* (stretching word)? (I record *o*.) /d/ like David? Okay, David can you help us record the *d*?"

Names on the Wall can be used for chunking, too. Consider the common chunks in J<u>ane</u>, Pet<u>er</u>, Fr<u>ank</u>, J<u>on</u>, Matth<u>ew</u>, Gr<u>ace</u>, Sh<u>ell</u>y, and Kell<u>y</u>.

Their Word Wall

Some teachers prefer building a Wall solely with words students request. The words can be listed in alphabetical order and used to make analogies to beginning sounds and common word chunks. As a writing workshop mini-lesson, students review their writing, looking for words requiring help. These are volunteered and written on cards. Teachers talk about the beginning sounds and helpful chunks as words are added to the Wall. For example, "Shandra needs help with *stand*. St-st-st-stand. *Stand* begins with s-t like *stop* and *steak*, and ends with a-n-d like *band*." The onset, or beginning sound(s), can be underlined in one color and the rime, or vowel chunk, in another color. Words requested during writing workshop may be written on cards and reviewed at the end of the writing session or other wordplay time.

Combination Word Wall

Some teachers prefer one Word Wall which combines the ABC Wall, the Words-We-Know Wall, and the Chunking Wall. Words are listed in alphabetical order and color coded. Irregular high-frequency words (words we know) are designated with a star or are written on yellow cards. Student's names and words with strong beginning sounds (ABC words) are written on green with onsets underlined. Words with good chunks (Chunk Wall words) are written on pink with chunks underlined. The same procedures are used for adding, reviewing, and making analogies to words on this space-saving Wall.

Using Walls in Limited Spaces

Many teachers have limited wall space or teach special groups (e.g., a.m. and p.m. kindergarten, resource groups). They often ask about alternative ways to build Word Walls. One way of beating the space problem is to build Word Walls on free-standing, three-paneled science boards typically used in science fairs. Science boards can be positioned on tables for everyone to see and moved freely around the room. They can be folded and removed. Different boards can be used to build Word Walls for different groups of students. Best of all, they don't take any wall space!

Manilla file folders make good Word Walls for individuals and small groups. Resource teachers or specialists can send students back to class with their folders to use throughout the day. Multi-age teachers might try file folders or science boards to meet the needs of varied groups.

Teaching Reading & Writing with Word Walls • Scholastic Professional Books

I also use my chalkboard space for Word Walls. Word cards are affixed to the board with sticky-tack. The cards can be removed and replaced without damaging the chalkboard surface.

Be creative! If Word Walls are a priority, you'll find space somewhere in your room. I've even seen Word Walls on classroom doors! Just be sure everyone can see the Wall and it can be referred to easily.

FINAL THOUGHTS

Word Walls are catching on—many teachers build them. The part often missing is constant real application—using the Walls in everyday reading and writing. Day-to-day modeling is key. Don't limit your Walls to tools for learning words or springboards for word-based activities or games. Use your Walls as references for skills and strategies *during* all kinds of reading and writing. When you demonstrate how to use skills and strategies in context, given the support of Word Walls, your students will succeed!

> *Teachers, researchers, parents, and the public agree that children need to develop and use what are sometimes called "basic skills," such as the ability to use phonics knowledge in reading, the ability to spell conventionally, and the ability to use grammatical constructions effectively . . . . What many people do not realize, however, is that the ability to use these skills is best fostered by teaching them in the context of their use. Research demonstrates that skills taught, practiced, and tested in isolation are not used as consistently or effectively as skills taught when children are actually reading and writing.* (Weaver, 1995 as cited in Routman, 1996, p. 199)

Learning in context is effective and *fun.* Starting from language that holds children's interest, like poems, rhymes, and chants, or their own news and stories, is motivating. I want my students to love reading and writing as much as I want them to be successful readers and writers. The excitement I see when I pick up a book to read aloud, the number of books checked out for home reading, the feverish pace of publishing, and the moans and groans I hear as we end writing work-shop are all important indicators of my students' motivation and the success of my teaching. And, I know I've met my goals when I receive end-of-year letters like this one from Annie, a kindergartner.

June 12, 1996

TO: Mrs. Wagstaff
Thank you for all you have done for me this school year.
The following is my gratitude and promise.

THANK YOU FOR TEACHING ME MY

A A
B B
C's C

THANK YOU FOR HELPING ME WITH MY

1
2
3's

BUT MOST OF ALL THANK YOU FOR HELPING ME
WITH *THE KEY TO SURVIVAL*, **READING!**

I can read
I like reading
I love reading
I will read the rest of the summer and forever!

Annie

A great Reader

P.S. My Family SAys THANK You Also!

Children's Literature

Belanger, C. (1988). *I Like the Rain.* Auckland, New Zealand: Shortland Publications.

Cannon, J. (1993). *Stellaluna.* San Diego, CA: Harcourt Brace.

Carter, D. A. (1991). *In a Dark, Dark Wood.* New York: Simon & Schuster.

Cowley, J. (1980). *Mrs. Wishy Washy.* Auckland, New Zealand: Shortland Publications.

Eastman, P. D. (1960). *Are You My Mother?* New York: Random House.

Fleming, D. (1992). *Lunch.* New York: Henry Holt.

Lawson, C. (1991). *Teddy Bear, Teddy Bear.* New York: Dial Books for Young Readers.

Martin, B. (1992). *Brown Bear, Brown Bear, What Do You See?* New York: Henry Holt.

Mayer, M. (1983). *I Was So Mad!* New York: Golden Books, Western Publishing.

Miranda, A. (1994). *Let's Get the Rhythm.* New York: Scholastic.

Munsch, R. N. (1980), *The Paper Bag Princess.* Toronto, Canada: Annick Press LTD.

Nayer, J. (1994). *A Tree Can Be.* New York: Scholastic.

Parish, P. (1979). *Amelia Bedelia.* New York: Greenwillow Books.

Peek, M. (1985). *Mary Wore Her Red Dress and Henry Wore His Green Sneakers.* New York: Clarion Books.

Peet, W. B. (1972). *The Ant and the Elephant.* Boston: Houghton Mifflin.

Prelutsky, J. (1984). *The New Kid on the Block.* New York: Greenwillow Books.

—. (1990). *Something Big Has Happened Here.* New York: Greenwillow Books.

—. (1996). *A Pizza the Size of the Sun.* New York: Greenwillow Books.

Rey, H. A. (1969). *Curious George.* Boston: Houghton Mifflin.

Sendak, M. (1963). *Where the Wild Things Are.* New York: Scholastic.

Silverstein, S. (1974). *Where the Sidewalk Ends.* New York: Harper and Row.

—. (1985). *A Light in the Attic.* New York: Harper and Row.

Stewig, J. W. (1991). *Stone Soup.* New York: Holiday House.

Suess, Dr. (1963). *Hop on Pop.* New York: Random House.

Wood, A. (1984). *The Napping House.* Orlando, FL: Harcourt Brace Jovanovich.

References

Adams, M. (1990). *Beginning to Read: Thinking and Learning About Print.* Cambridge, MA: MIT Press.

Anderson, R. C., Hiebert, E. H., Scott, J. A., & Wilkinson, I. A. G. (1985) *Becoming a Nation of Readers: The Report of the Commission on Reading.* Champaign, IL: Center for the Study of Reading: Washington, DC: National Institute of Education.

Brown, K. J., Sinatra, G. M., & Wagstaff, J. M. (1996). "Exploring the Potential of Analogy Instruction to Support Students' Spelling Development." *The Elementary School Journal,* 97, 81–99.

Cambourne, B. (1988). *The Whole Story: Natural Learning and the Acquisition of Literacy in the Classroom.* Richmond Hill, Ontario: Scholastic–TAB.

——. (1995). "Toward an Educationally Relevant Theory of Literacy Learning: Twenty Years of Inquiry." *The Reading Teacher,* 49, 182–190.

Clay, M. M. (1980). *The Early Detection of Reading Difficulties.* Portsmouth, NH: Heinemann.

——. (1991). *Becoming Literate: The Construction of Inner Control.* Portsmouth, NH: Heinemann.

——. (1993). *Reading Recovery: A Guidebook for Teachers in Training.* Portsmouth, NH: Heinemann.

——. (1993). *An Observation Survey of Early Literacy Achievement.* Portsmouth, NH: Heinemann.

Cunningham, P. M. (1995). *Phonics They Use: Words for Reading and Writing.* (2nd Ed.) New York: HarperCollins College Publisher.

Downer, M. A. & Gaskins, I. W. (1986). *Benchmark Word Identification/Vocabulary Development Program.* Media, PA: Benchmark Press.

Elkonin, D. B. (1973), "Methods of Teaching Reading: USSR. In J. Downing" (Ed.), *Comparative Reading: Cross-National Studies of Behavior and Processes in Reading and Writing* (pp. 551–580). New York: Macmillan.

Fountas, I. C. & Pinnell, G. S. (1996). *Guided Reading: Good First Teaching for All Children.* Portsmouth, NH: Heinemann.

Fry, E. (1998). "The Most Common Phonograms." *The Reading Teacher,* 51, 620–622.

——. (1998). *Phonics Patterns: Onset and Rhyme Word Lists.* Laguna Beach, CA: Laguna Beach Educational Books.

Gambrell, L. B. (1996). "Creating Classroom Cultures That Foster Reading Motivation." *The Reading Teacher,* 50, 14–25.

Gaskins, R. W., Gaskins, J. C., & Gaskins, I. W. (1991). "A Decoding Program for Poor Readers—And the Rest of the Class, Too!" *Language Arts,* 68, 213–225.

——. (1992). "Using What You Know to Figure Out What You Don't Know: An Analogy Approach to Decoding." *Reading and Writing Quarterly,* 8, 197–221.

Gaskins, I. W., Ehri, L. C., Cress, C., O'Hara, C., & Donnelly, K. (1997). "Procedures for Word Learning: Making Discoveries About Words." *The Reading Teacher,* 50, 312–327.

Gaskins, I. W. (1998). "There's More to Teaching At-Risk and Delayed Readers Than Good Reading Instruction." *The Reading Teacher,* 51, 534–547.

Guthrie, J. T. & Wigfield, A. (1997). *Reading Engagement: Motivating Readers Through Integrated Instruction.* Newark, DE: International Reading Association.

Hayward, C. C. (1998). "Monitoring Spelling Development." *The Reading Teacher,* 51, 444–445.

Mooney, M. E. (1990). *Reading To, With, and By Children.* Katonah, NY: Richard C. Owen Publishers, Inc.

Moustafa, M. (1997). *Beyond Traditional Phonics: Research Discoveries and Reading Instruction.* Portsmouth, NH: Heinemann.

Pinnell, G. S. & McCarrier, A. (1994). "Interactive Writing: A Transitional Tool for Assisting Children in Learning to Read and Write." In E. Hiebert & B. Taylor (Eds.), *Getting Reading Right from the Start: Effective Early Literacy Interventions* (pp. 149–170). Needham, MA: Allyn & Bacon.

Routman, R. (1991). *Invitations: Changing as Teachers and Learners K–12.* Portsmouth, NH: Heinemann.

——. (1996). *Literacy at the Crossroads: Crucial Talk about Reading, Writing, and Other Teaching Dilemmas.* Portsmouth, NH: Heinemann.

——. (1996). "Reclaiming the Basics." *Instructor,* 105 (8),49–54.

Sitton, R. (1996). "Achieving Spelling Literacy: A No-Excuses Approach." *The California Readers,* 30 (1), 5–7.

——. (1996). *Rebecca Sitton's Spelling Sourcebook 1.* Portland, OR: Northwest Textbook.

——. (1998). *Increasing Student Spelling Achievement in Daily Writing Across the Curriculum.* (9th Ed.) Portland, OR: Northwest Textbook.

Snow, C. E., Burns, M. S., Griffin, P. Eds. (1998). *Preventing Reading Difficulties in Young Children.* Washington, DC: National Academy Press.

Stahl, S. A. (1992). "Saying the "p" Word: Nine Guidelines for Exemplary Phonics Instruction." *The Reading Teacher,* 45, 618–626.

Squire, J. R. (1994). "Consensus Emerging, but a Way to Go." In Lehr, F. & Osborn, J. (Eds.) *Reading, Language, and Literacy: Instruction for the Twenty-First Century* (pp. 283–286). Hillsdale, NJ: Lawrence Erlbaum Associates.

Strickland, D. S. (1990). "Emergent Literacy: How Young Children Learn to Read." *Educational Leadership,* March, 18–23.

Strickland, D. S. (1998). *Teaching Phonics Today: A Primer for Educators.* Newark, DE: International Reading Association.

Vacca, J. L., Vacca, R. T., & Gove, M. K. (1995). *Reading and Learning to Read.* New York: HarperCollins.

Wagstaff, J. M. (1994). *Phonics That Work: New Strategies for the Reading/Writing Classroom.* New York: Scholastic.

Wagstaff, J. M. & Sinatra, G. M. (1995). "Promoting Efficient and Independent Word Recognition: A New Strategy for Readers and Writers." *Balanced Reading Instruction,* 2, 27–37.

Wagstaff, J. M. (1997). "Building Practical Knowledge of Letter-Sound Correspondences: A Beginner's Word Wall and Beyond." *The Reading Teacher,* 51, 298–304.

Weaver, C. (1995). "Facts on Teaching Skills in Context." In Weaver, C., Gillmeister-Krause, L., & Vento-Zogby, G. *Creating Support for Effective Literacy Education.* Portsmouth, NH: Heinemann.

Wylie, R. & Durrell, D. (1970). "Teaching Vowels Through Phonograms." *Elementary English,* 47, 787–791.

NOTES